FIRST PRESBYTERIAN
CHURCH
ROYAL OAK

In Honor of
Ruth and Tom
Kirkman

Given by

Youth Elders

1984

THE REAL WORLD OF THE
IMPRESSIONISTS

THE REAL WORLD OF THE
IMPRESSIONISTS

Paintings and Photographs 1848-1918

YANN LE PICHON

Translated by Dianne Cullinane

HARRISON HOUSE
New York

CONTENTS

Honoré Daumier: **The Politics of Beer Drinkers.**

FOREWORD

IN THIS BOOK YANN LE PICHON invites us to follow him into the open-air cafes, inns and cabarets where countless painters once found a refuge from the anxieties and physical miseries that all too often were their lot. Camaraderie and wine helped them first to laugh at the myopia of the society in which they found themselves, and then to discover the competitive spirit that painters always need to reinvent art.

There is a sadness in some of the faces collected here: faces lost in thought, exchanging anxious glances or staring moodily into a mauve-tinted glass of absinthe, a tint we see as well in the seascapes of Odilon Redon. But these are fleeting images surrounded by scenes of joy: the burst of laughter at the dance, the boating parties, the rambling country walks and fervent talks before the fire. Altogether these moments show us that what writer Henri Murger called "the dog's life" was equally a life dedicated to pleasure. In the end, pleasure redeemed it all.

The vision of happiness that is celebrated in these canvases is not a simple hedonism, but a kind of salvation wrested from the *work* of art that offered the artist some compensation for the painful dramas in his life. Van Gogh's suicide, Gauguin's solitude, Sisley's misery—all remind us of the suffering of painters in a world contradictory enough to have showered gold and medals on its favorite artists. When we read the correspondence of the artists themselves, or the novels of the era whose protagonists were painters—Zola's *l'Œuvre* and the Goncourt brothers' *Manette Salomon*—we sense the depth of the misery and hopelessness that haunted them. In Murger's *Scenes from a Bohemian Life,* the hero "Petit Gris" inhabits a tiny fifth floor room where beaten earth covers the floor and light filters in through oiled paper. In Zola's *l'Œuvre* the painter Claude Lantier, who is none other than Cézanne, remarks that whether he "lunches or dines matters little, for the menu is always the same, vermicelli and a mash of bread dipped in oil, country style."

An even harsher reality is depicted by the Goncourts' description of Daumier, who lives "in a room crammed with men who sat huddled on the floor around a steaming pot, drinking their wine directly from the bottle." To the "Brothers" these painters who consumed *vin ordinaire*—"for [them] all wine was the same"—seemed almost proletarian. Together with Zola they lamented the poverty of taste of "young men born with just enough breeding to stay afloat."

In the work of Teniers, Brouwer, Leprince, Millet, Modigliani and Soutine, one does indeed find images of an insistant and endless misery, a destitution that would be intolerable were it not tempered by the human warmth these painters seemed to find nowhere more than in the cafes. Whether it was Le Guerbois, Les Canotiers or La Rotonde, the cafe was the poor man's salon. It was only at the tavern, for example, that the Dutchman, Teniers, found the warmth of the hearth and the heart. With his canvas propped up in one corner, Teniers combed this wild and thirsty world in the hope that one of its more fortunate customers would be tempted to buy the work of one less sober than he.

The cafe was also the Academy. The cafe Guerbois welcomed the meetings of the Impressionists. In such a place plums were preserved in brandy, but also traditions. Consider the Surrealist André Breton who as late as 1970 could be found holding court with his followers every evening at five o'clock at a bistro a few steps from the Paris Stock Exchange.

No wonder then that these humble taverns and dance halls became the vulcan forges for the birth of a new kind of painting. The great movements of French painting erupted from historic battlegrounds as different as the Revolution of 1848 and the first World War, but as the multitude of images in this book reminds us, they also sprang from the hunger for companionship and recognition that led so many painters to create a world apart from the turmoil around them.

Turning the pages of this book, we learn something else about the painting of the era. Moving from Corot, the great ancestor of modern painting, to the naturalist Théodore Rousseau, on through the Impressionists—the ultimate representatives of a Rubenesque world—we begin to appreciate how the art of painting holds its ground against time, even against the compartmentalization of Naturalism, Impressionism, Pointilism, Fauvism and Cubism.

Happiness! Yann Le Pichon is right to invoke this theme. In the end perhaps we should not look for darker meanings in the melancholy expression worn by Manet's *Boatman,* or linger too long with Lautrec's drinking women, or wonder at their haggard faces, the same face that is turned toward Picasso when he paints Fernande in the cafe. Instead let us accept the astonishing bouquet which Yann Le Pichon presents us, one that combines thistles and roses in such abundance that we can no more tire of examining it than we can stop being charmed and intrigued by the universe of painting.

by Maurice Rheims
The French Academy

Pablo Picasso: **Composition of Bread and Fruit on a Table** (1909).

INTRODUCTION

IN *THE REAL WORLD OF THE IM-PRESSIONISTS* I have chosen to revisit—with the help of Editions Laffont's active staff—the birthplaces of the grand and beautiful body of painting born in France between 1848 and 1918. My purpose is not to compare the work of art with its natural setting, nor to analyze pictorial technique, but to recreate the intimate milieus that shaped the vision of Impressionism.

In keeping with *The Sources of Art,* the series of which this book is a part, *The Real World of the Impressionists* leads us backward from the masterpieces themselves to the circumstances of their creation. Having renounced official art and the routines of academicism, the Impressionist painters ventured forth like pioneers to the countryside, the sea, and the humblest—but also the liveliest—quarters of Paris. Accordingly, each of the six chapters in the book is set in one of these extraordinary environments where painters gathered to draw inspiration from each other and from the peculiar ambiance of the place.

If there is a single experience common to the places where the Impressionists worked it is that the great discoveries of the period came to light in modest inns and bistros, open-air cafes and cabarets. Here was where the most inventive and influential masters met, encouraged and through an irrepressible rebelliousness, liberated each other. The artists who banded together in these settings found the double happiness of fraternity warmed by wine, to be sure, and innovation.

Today we take pleasure in the individual paintings that testify to this grand adventure. Why not share the happy circumstances that surrounded their creation as well? In so doing perhaps we can penetrate one of the mysteries of art: perhaps we can reenter the intimate world of the painters themselves.

My own imagination was siezed by this possibility quite by chance during a visit to Honfleur four years ago. I was seated on the terrace at Saint-Siméon, the farm where a good many Impressionist painters used to take their meals. It was a clear spring morning and the terrace was filled with flowers, open and gay like the terrace that Monet painted at Sainte-Adresse. The apple trees had begun to shed their petals, which filled the air like low-flying clouds. As I sipped my cider the farm's manager quietly joined me, and his friendly smile prompted me to speak. "Eugene Boudin and his friends brought me to this place," I told him. "It is so full of their spirits that I have begun to see everything through their eyes."

I felt as if I had awakened from a happy dream at dawn only to find that the sensations of the dream, the color and light of Saint-Siméon, were quite present. The painters I loved had actually eaten their breakfasts at these same wooden tables where we sat. "They spread their bread with Mother Toutain's golden butter," I laughed, "and snacked on shrimp washed down with her husband's sparkling cider." The manager was amused. "Do you know that my American, English, German, Japanese and even French and Belgian guests who come here from the Landing Beach in Normandy are more curious about the painters who worked here than about World War II," he said. "I need a brochure to answer all their questions. There's no book about their years here."

It was true. These painters had earned a reputation as glorious as that of the Allies: art outlasts war, death and the test of time. And so it was that the idea for this book came to me and its first images invaded my mind. As I sat on that terrace I thought of all the artists who had sat there before me, and my head filled with visions of farms and inns, rivers and forests, open-air cafes and brasseries, Montmartre and Montparnasse—all the places where the young artists who gathered to reinvent art shared happiness and friendship.

I looked across at the barn that Monet had painted in 1867 when it was covered with snow. On its roof perched two perfectly white Picasso doves; like the image of the pigeons in La Fontaine, I imagined them rising in flight toward the chapel of Notre-Dame de Grâce, the inspiration of so many of the delicate drawings, watercolors and canvases that I held before my eyes because I had them in my heart.

What power of evocation and crystallization did these painters possess that enabled them to transmit their marvelous visions of nature and of man? Where did they find the gift of second sight with which they managed to outwit death and the passing of time? Today their vision of this countryside is imbedded in our consciousness, sometimes without our even knowing it.

Who can pass along the Côte de Grâce without seeing Boudin's canvases in the cloud-scattered skies, or stroll along the beach at Étretat and not think of Courbet or Monet? Who can explore the forest of Fontainebleau without evoking Théodore Rousseau or Jean-François Millet? And who does not imagine himself in the company of Pissarro, Sisley or Seurat when watching a canoe drift by on the Seine's current or a barge pass through a lock?

The shadows of the great painters pass over the places they inhabited and seem to haunt us when we visit these spots in a certain mood. Like visitors from imperishable books who suddenly reappear when we visit the places where they dwelled in literature, the Impressionists return to us in Honfleur, Chailly-en-Bière, Barbizon, Pont-Aven, Montmartre, Montparnasse. Their art dwells within us and changes us without our knowledge, like the "reawakened archetypes" which Jung believed inhabited our collective unconscious. Nothing confirms this better than advertising. How many boxes of chocolates or *marrons glacés* owe their consumption to Renoir's plump and appetizing young women? How many mugs of beer have been drunk at the instigation of those happy people bathed in Impressionist sunlight? How many dresses or pieces of jewelry by famous designers are derived from Cubist or abstract paintings?

"Painting must aim at universality," advised Leonardo da Vinci. How many expressions remind us of the *Mona Lisa?* In how many homes has Millet's *Angelus* silently sounded? And how many young lovers, even those in jeans, have dreamed of the Moulin de la Galette?

"In painting, a mysterious bridge is established between the soul of the figures and that of the spectator," said Delacroix. Between painters and their models, as well, are these bridges created, and among artists themselves, one might add. To create the bridges that lead us back to the geographical, sociological, historical and deeply emotional origins of Impressionism—that is the task of this book.

Yann Le Pichon

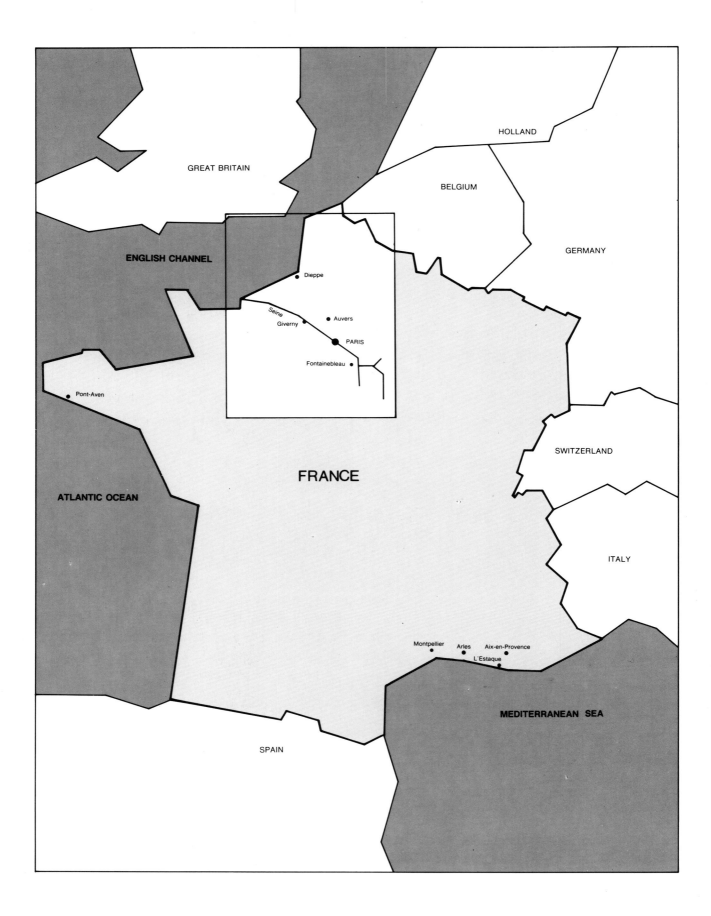

HOLLAND

GREAT BRITAIN

BELGIUM

ENGLISH CHANNEL

GERMANY

Dieppe

Seine
Auvers
Giverny
PARIS

Fontainebleau

SWITZERLAND

Pont-Aven

ATLANTIC OCEAN

FRANCE

ITALY

Montpellier
Arles
Aix-en-Provence
L'Estaque

MEDITERRANEAN SEA

SPAIN

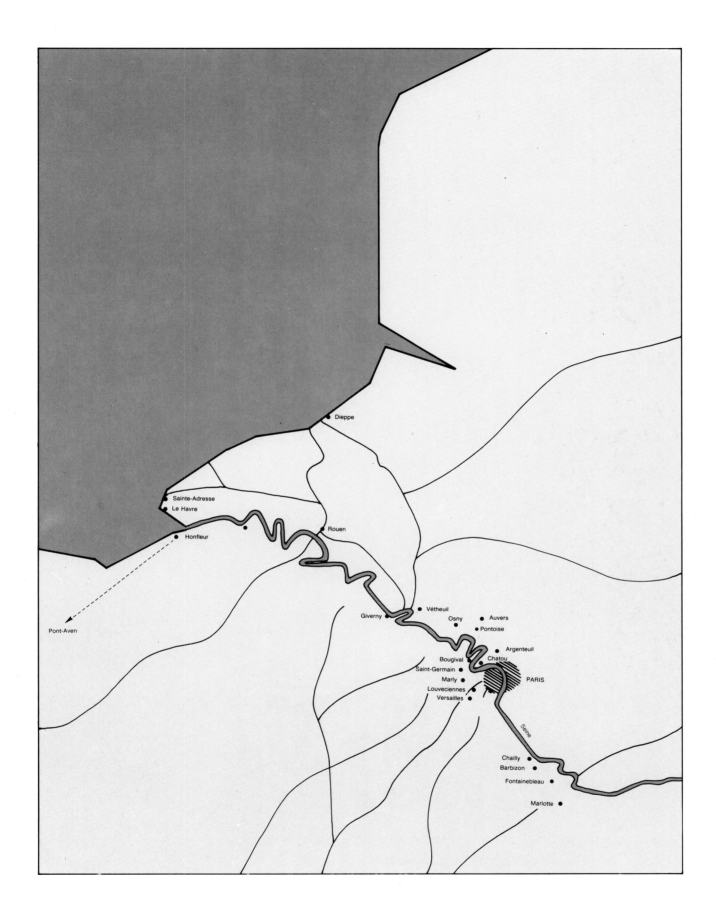

Dieppe

Sainte-Adresse
Le Havre

Honfleur

Rouen

Pont-Aven

Vétheuil
Giverny   Osny   Auvers
                      Pontoise

                        Argenteuil
            Bougival   Chatou
Saint-Germain
      Marly   PARIS
   Louveciennes
   Versailles

                          Seine

               Chailly
            Barbizon
         Fontainebleau

               Marlotte

19

1
BARBIZON
CHAILLY-EN-BIÈRE
Return to the Earth

Gustave Courbet: **The Meeting or Bonjour, Monsieur Courbet.**

As THE STAGECOACH THAT drove him to the countryside moves off into the distance, Gustave Courbet, the master of Realism, receives the deferential greeting of his friend Albert Bruyas. In this symbolic meeting between artist and patron, Courbet depicts himself as a sort of wandering Bohemian, whose path toward the future is being opened up by Bruyas' welcoming gesture. "Good morning, Mr. Courbet," says Bruyas. "Long live friendship and liberty!" is Courbet's triumphant response.

This self-portrait typifies the daring approach taken after the Revolution of 1848 (three days of violent insurrection leading to the downfall of King Louis Philippe and the formation of the Second Republic) by those painters who were bored by the historical and religious themes of Romanticism. Returning to the earth and to naturalism, they were rebelling against the constraints of their Parisian studios as well as their servitude to the Salon's conservative clientele. This painting, in which the artist turns his back on the spectator, can also be seen as a farewell to the Academy of Painting and Sculpture, whose rigid hierarchy established accepted artistic standards.

Gustave Courbet: **The Meeting or Bonjour, Monsieur Courbet.** Detail (1854).

"Why should I search for what doesn't exist in the world and disfigure what I find by efforts of the imagination?" Courbet asks. "The beauty of nature is superior to all art's conventions," to all the artifices used by official artists whose compromises have been bought by the affluent bourgeoisie.

Courbet wanted to "lower the tone" of painting and suggested that his comrades "paint only what they can see." Those who followed his advice shocked the official art world. Count Nieuwerkerke, the Imperial Superintendent of Fine Arts, described their paintings as "the painting of democrats, of those who don't change their clothes and who want to impose themselves on mankind..."

The artists defended themselves against these charges: "It's through you that the People will find their voice," Michelet wrote to Daumier in 1851. "I was born a peasant, I shall remain a peasant," Millet explained to Delacroix in 1853. "To the devil with the the civilized world. Long live Nature and Poetry!" was Théodore Rousseau's defiant rejoinder.

This new breed of artists shared the desire to escape from the tyranny of the fashionable world. They needed to find a place where they could realize their dream of a new art. They searched for a setting in which they could reconcile art with the real world, which was free and generous—no longer bogged down in the past or stuffy bourgeoise tastes. Where could they go to find this freedom?

Art and Society

Meeting at literary cafés such as the *Andler* brasserie, these artists held passionate discussions on the social relevance and destiny of art. They shared their views with poets like Baudelaire, writers such as Champfleury and philosophers such as Proudhon. There was much debate over the insurrectional tendencies of these thinkers, whose polemics were sometimes too radical for the painters. Where else did these artists look for inspiration?

They looked to Italy where Corot in particular found an earthly paradise lost in the pure visions of Italian primitivism. Equal inspiration was found in the 17th century Dutch masters, such as Ruisdael, Hobbema or Van Goyen, whose luminous landscapes hung in the Louvre. Important, too, was the English and Norman influence, where the clear and vaporous visions of Bonington and Constable, made them aware of how cold, dry and cerebral French art had become.

When they traveled—as Courbet and Troyon did to the Netherlands—the journey only made them realize that what they were seeking could be found in their own country, even within the gates of Paris. They discovered that the return to the limitless beauty of the Earth began in their own eyes.

Poets and writers proclaimed the beauty of nature and man's quest for innocence and purity. Victor Hugo wrote Odes marveling at the beauty and simplicity of rural life. The artists read George Sand's novels and were attracted to the countryside where man was depicted as one with the elements. They were impressed by Alfred de Musset's account of his bucolic love affair with Sand in the forest of Fontainebleau in 1833, as told in *Confessions of a Child of the Century*.

They passed on the word: Fontainebleau. It was the 'Open Sesame!' for painting. From Fontainebleau's rocks and in the shade of its caves they saw color scattered across the soil, climbing the trees, filtering through the foliage and tinting the atmosphere. Their affinity for this ancient forest resembled that of Flaubert's heroes in *Sentimental Education*. Rosanette and Frédéric fled Paris in the midst of the 1848 Revolution and encountered a blue smocked painter working at the foot of an oak tree. Flaubert describes this couple's reaction and enchantment with Fontainebleau.

The ambition of these artists was to become rustic painters. They wanted to plant their easels in the ground and hang their palettes on the branches. They rose at dawn in order to catch the sparkle of sunlight in the morning dew and worked until twilight so that they could retain the earth's tones as seen throughout the day. They found that everything they saw in these surroundings merited the precise lines of their pencils, followed by the careful delineation of their brushes.

In this forest, flocks of predatory and multicolored birds darted and ricocheted among the ancient oaks and tall beech trees. Wide paths emerged onto heath-carpeted clearings where stags confronted one another. Disorderly hordes of pine trees surrounded a vast chaos of sandstone speckled with gold and grey-green lichen. After François I, the kings of France preferred this forest above all others for the hunt. It also became the first and largest studio for landscape and wildlife painters of the 19th century. Barbizon would become the center of this school, with Chailly-en-Bière and Marlotte as extensions.

These woods were once the home of woodcutters and gleaners. They were also a refuge for gamekeepers and furtive poachers, smugglers and outlaws. King Louis XVI, returning from a hunt, was heard to remark "The only things I saw in the forest were wild boars and Brunandet." Brunandet (1755-1804), condemned to death for having pushed an unfaithful companion out of a window, established his hideout in the forest. Here he made the woods his model and painting his mistress. "The thrust of a sword is nothing. It's much more difficult to stroke in a tree or a blue sky," he confided to a fellow artist. Canvases were already beginning to exhale the musky and mossy scent of the underbrush.

Stamati Bulgari, a student of Jacques Louis David, recorded his astonishment at seeing one of the early open air landscape painters during his stay at an inn at Chailly-en-Bière. He described the artist: "A grey canvas blouse served him as both a smock and brush-rag; spats and military boots with large snaps protected his thin legs and delicate feet; his chair was held together by an old belt; in one hand, he held a large canvas, while the other contained a pike to fasten his sunshade. He carried a haversac on his back, along with his paint box and easel." This was in 1821 and Bulgari himself, armed with a sword and accompanied by his valet, soon aroused the curiosity of travelers, hunters and farmers.

The first stop on the way south from Paris, Chailly was the last village before penetrating that new "promised land," of which Barbizon, with its privileged location in the midst of the forest, was the capital.

Some sixty or so simple thatched cottages lined the muddy street that emerged directly into the Bas-Bréau and the forest. These cottages, dotted with wallflowers and irises, housed the woodcutters, coalmen, quarry workers and gamekeepers who made up the scant population of Barbizon. This quaint and excellently situated village attracted many young artists who, because of their beards, were nicknamed 'Buffaloes.' The taciturn locals congregated at *père* Ganne's over a pint, while their wives stored up on supplies and gossip at the grocery run by Mrs. Ganne.

François Ganne soon saw that these artists needed food and lodging and turned his pub into an inn. He hung up the symbolic juniper branch and persuaded his wife to become the cook. Her steaming pots of soup simmering on the stove, geese roasting on the spit and ripe Brie cheeses, provided nourishment for the hungry artists. In order to pay for their supper, or just for fun, these artists brightened the walls, sideboards and dividing panels with their sketches.

Rising well before dawn, Mrs. Ganne, her dog Ronflot at her heels, prepared the artists' picnics. She filled their straw baskets with hearty slices of bread, hard boiled eggs, chicken drumsticks, Brie, apples and bottles of wine. She then sent them off into the woods like messengers of the "Bethlehem of modern painting" as Jules Breton called it. Local shepherds and milkmaids served as their guides, leading them along the forest paths or through neighboring fields.

Pilgrim-painters of the forest, they considered it as their own. "To paint a country, you must know it," maintained Courbet. They strove to paint 'on the spot' throughout the day, storing their equipment in the rocks if they had not finished their compositions by the day's end. It was important for them to echo nature's processes "through alluviums which, united or piled on top of each other, become the forces and transparencies," observed Théodore Rousseau. But their fear of imitation ("Don't change the position of a branch, God put it there on purpose," advised Corot) was not exaggerated. They still had an ardent desire for personal expression derived from the contemplation of nature. "We should believe in the first impression. If we have really been touched, our emotion will show," suggested Corot.

Attentive to harmony and the power and richness of tonality, the painters applied themselves to capturing what Rousseau called the "airy relief" and what Millet termed as "the atmospheric covering of things." These preoccupations with atmospheric effects were indispensable discoveries pre-figuring Impressionism. A sort of rivalry was established between these painters. In the evenings they initiated newcomers by making them smoke a pipe and judged by the smoke rings whether they were "classicists" or, preferably, "colorists." When weather permitted they made nocturnal excursions into the forest where they continued their discussions on the color and form of beauty and the effects of light and shadow. Their pantheism led sometimes to fiery outbursts and quarrels between the more obstinant adherents.

Finally, to take full advantage of "the particular calmness exuded by large forests, like a cathedral's shadow spread out over the surrounding buildings" (E. and J. Goncourt), an entire galaxy of painters became more or less permanently installed at Fontainebleau. These artists included Barye, Babcock, Bodmer, Chaigneau, Diaz, Gassies, Grigoresco, Laveille, Millet, Olivier de Penne, Rousseau and Ziem. They established roots at Barbizon—some of them, such as Rousseau and Millet, until their deaths—renting, buying or exchanging houses with one another. Some adopted the life of the villagers. Charles Jacque, for example, attempted to raise domestic fowl and asparagus. In 1872, Barbizon contained 147 villagers plus a hundred or so French and foreign artists.

In their novel *Manette Salomon* (1867), the Goncourt brothers described the productive and fraternal life of the landscape painters who flocked to Barbizon beginning in 1848. Indeed, the Revolution of 1848 marked a decisive turning point in French social and artistic history, Proudhon had just published *System of Economic Contradictions; or The Philosophy of Poverty,* and Marx and Engels' *Communist Manifesto* had also appeared.

This was the beginning of an awareness of the social upheavals caused by the Industrial Revolution, whose unrelenting caricaturist was Honoré Daumier. This was also the time when a naturalist movement was born from the experimental sciences and the positivism of Auguste Comte. Artists, writers and philosophers were now turning from the subject to the object, from dreams to concrete reality, from the imaginary to faithful description.

In 1847 Delacroix wrote in his journal that his aim was to "produce paintings that would have all the freedom and freshness of sketches." And Théodore Rousseau said that "our art is only capable of attaining the sublime through exact truth." Artists were leaving behind the supernatural which had been mummified by academic art and turning to the unadulterated depiction of nature.

In Harmony with the Environment

There were other factors that accounted for the regrouping of these new realists around Barbizon. Beginning in 1849, trains ran from Paris to Fontainebleau, enabling the artists to make the journey in an hour and a half. In addition, their equipment became lighter: the availability of paint in tubes eliminated the cumbersome pre-mixing of pigments; while the invention of folding easels made it easier to work out of doors. Finally, the outbreak of cholera caused a major exodus from Paris. Among those fleeing the city was Jean-François Millet. Encouraged by his friend Charles Jacque, Millet joined him at 42 rue Rochechouart where Jacque lived with a group of artists. Millet fell in love with "the trees and rocks, the flight of black crows over the plains, the rooftops whose chimneys emit whirls of smoke which unfurl poetically, as the women prepare supper for the weary souls returning from the fields." From his surroundings Millet extracted lively pastoral elegies, bathed in such timeless light that they will always move us, in the same way that they moved Van Gogh, Pissarro, Seurat and Gauguin.

Van Gogh found that the Barbizon artists had made a very noble conquest, that of an "art which comforts." Their works, the fruit of revolutionary as well as peaceful intentions were, in both Realist and Romantic degrees, the debut of one of the most important developments in painting: Impressionism. Following in their footsteps through this same inspired forest, Cézanne, Monet, Renoir, Bazille and Sisley eventually overtook them on their quest for light and the joy of living in harmony with nature.

Caruelle d'Aligny: **View of the Quarries of Mont-Saint-Père in Fontainebleau Forest.**

Caruelle d'Aligny, one of Corot's companions in Rome, revealed to him the splendor and mystery of Fontainebleau—from its rocky deserts to its deep woods. D'Aligny was one of the first guests at Ganne's inn, before moving to nearby Marlotte. Quitting Paris and turning his back on the past, d'Aligny chose the painstaking work of painting on the spot with a naturalist's precision. Using this technique he sought to capture the real, untamed tonalities of the landscape.

Corot was also interested in depicting nature's true colors. In his sketch **Fontainebleau, route to Orléans,** he even went as far as writing in the colors as he found them, "golden tree, dark heath and terrain, soiled yellow, dark copper." He wanted to show that "beneath the foliage everything is full of spirits" and found subaqueous and coralline tints in Fontainebleau's irregular, glacially sculpted sandstone. As early as 1834, he was advising novice painters to "Draw firmly and truthfully, concentrate on what's before you and the true aspect of the color will emerge from the eye."

Auguste Anastasi:
**Fontainebleau Forest:
Wolves Gorge** (1858).

Camille Corot:
**Fontainebleau:
Road to Orléans.**

Camille Corot: **Rocks in Fontainebleau Forest.**

The Fairy Oaks. Fontainebleau forest (photo).

Painters on the rocks at Fontainebleau (photo).

Portrait of Théodore Rousseau.
Attributed to Honoré Daumier.

Théodore Rousseau: **The Roche Oak** (May 1861).

Less sociable and communicative than Corot, Théodore Rousseau was depicted by Daumier as a fierce personality. However, although he may have been as upright and obstinate as **The Roche Oak** with which he identifies in his etching of that title, Rousseau had many solid friendships. Among his friends were Jean-François Millet (whom he was buried beside at Chailly) and Diaz de la Pena, whom he knew from his Paris days. Despite shared views on nature, Diaz and Rousseau's paintings were quite dissimilar. Whereas Rousseau chose subdued colors in achieving nature's effects, Diaz used bold tones to create dramatic contrasts.

Alexandre Véron's sketches of Wolve's Gorge testify to the 'truant spirit' of these painters. Their rendezvous directly with nature were their adieux from Fontainebleau to the dictatorial academicism of the Salon.

Rousseau's Roche Oak (photo).

Narcisse Diaz de la Pena: **Rocks at Fontainebleau, Beautiful Pine** (c. 1840–45).

Camille Corot: **Self Portrait.**

Alexandre Véron: **Millet, Rousseau and Véron at Wolves Gorge.**

Olivier de Penne:
The Festival of Barbizon.

The Ganne Inn Museum (contemporary photo).

Xavier de Cock:
**Portraits of
Mr. and Mrs. Ganne**
(1854).

Decorative
panel from
Ganne Inn.

Barbizon stagecoach (photo).

When François Ganne and his wife noticed the arrival in Barbizon of young artists, exhilarated and ravenous after their outings in the forest, they decided to open a combination inn and grocery in 1822. They gradually added rooms on the ground floor which served not only as a pension for the artists but also offered them the opportunity to "drain off their overly full palettes" onto the dividing walls and furniture. As a result, Corot, Rousseau, Diaz, Huet and Nanteuil, among others, transformed the inn into what an 1853 issue of Illustration magazine called a palace worthy of comparison with a Florentine villa.

The artists led a hearty and rustic life, participating in village festivities and making the most of their forays into the forest. They often took père Ganne along with them on their lively ramblings. His picnic basket on his shoulder, he urged his favorites onto the rocks, while chasing the "classical" painters like dogs, since they were unworthy of the brotherhood of "colorists."

Decorative panel from Ganne Inn.

Charles Jacque: **Entrance to Ganne's Inn.**

Inner farmyard.

Decorative panels illustrated by Théodore Rousseau, Diaz, Nanteuil, Jadin and Perrin.

Charcoal drawings of Mr. and Mrs. Ganne (anonymous).

Olivier de Penne: **The Wedding Dinner** (c. 1859).

Nom de Famille	Prénoms	Age	Profession	Lieu de Naissance	Domi Commune
Cambon	Charles	46	artiste peintre	Paris	
Guillemin	Alexandre	30	Artiste id	Paris	Paris
Thirry	Joseph	35	Dito	Paris	Paris
Rousseau	Théodore		Artiste	Paris	Paris
Cambon			Artiste	Paris	Paris
Schaffers	Nestor	27	artiste	Liége	id
Xavier De Cock	Xavier	24	artiste	Gand	id
Demartelaere	Luig	32	artiste	Gand	id
Schmit Grand	Michiel	23	Artiste	Rotterdam	
T. Seggers	Floder	26		Amsterdam	
Bruning	Nicolaas		Particulier	Rotterdam	
Mercereau	Charles	29	artiste	Rochefort	id
Thiebault	Julien	17	étudiant	Paris	id
Morvin	Armand	24	Artiste	Paris	id
Hoelzaral	Charles	28	Artiste	Paris	id
Barye	antoine Louis	57	sculpteur	Paris	id
Daumier	Honoré	44	artiste peintre	Marseille	id
Sutter	David	37	artiste	Paris	id
Zier	Félix	30	artiste peintre	Beaune	id

The Guest Register from Ganne Inn (1848).

In 1859 Louise Ganne married a young painter named Eugène Cuvelier. Corot was a witness and the life of the party. Other guests included Rousseau and Millet who joined in singing the chorus of the famous lament of Barbizon, "The painters of Barbizon paint like Buffalo." This event was celebrated by Olivier de Penne in his **Wedding Dinner.**

Barbizon became increasingly popular with artists; the annual police register listed 28 in residence as early as 1848. In 1870 Edmond Luniot, the Ganne's son-in-law, opened another artists' inn. He and his wife furnished their inn with furniture and panels (photographed here for the first time) from the Ganne Inn. The perfect trompe-l'œil of some of the panels calls to mind Courbet's words: "I would like to eat my painting."

Anonymous illustration in the Guest register at Ganne Inn (1876).

board door Ganne Inn.

Decorated door.

"The painter's bacchanal."

upboard.

Trompe-l'œil on sideboard.

33

Camille Corot: **Stamati Bulgari at work,**
"in a fury of reason" (c. 1835).

Charles Sauvageot: **The Artist's Inn at Barbizon**
(**Illustration,** March, 13, 1875)

L iving in daily contact with the farmers and their animals (as portrayed by Charles Jacque) the new realists developed a rural patience and discovered the regulating role of the sun and the moon. They were also drawn by the farmers' sensitivity to atmospheric phenomena and inspired by their capacity for resignation.

Said Corot, for whom painting was a serious and risky child's game, "I am always trying to see the immediate effect. I am like a child who blows a soap bubble; at first it is small but already spherical; then he blows again, but quite cautiously, until he fears that it will explode. I work on all parts of a canvas at the same time, carefully perfecting them until I have found the total effect. I begin, therefore, with the shaded areas and this makes sense. Since this is what strikes you the most, it must be rendered first."

Charles Jacque: **Farmyard.**

Camille Corot's notes on painting.

34

Camille Corot: **Farmyard at Fontainebleau** (c. 1860–65).

Corot painting (photo).

Camille Corot:
**Boy Wearing
a Tall Hat Seated
on the Ground.**

35

The Théodore
Rousseau Museum
(contemporary photo).

Interior of
Théodore Rousseau's
studio.

Photographic portrait of Théodore Rousseau.

Georges Gassies: **Théodore Rousseau's House in Barbizon.**

Georges Gassies: **Self Portrait.**

Théodore Rousseau: **Fontainebleau Forest, Winter Sunset** (c. 1846).

*S*addened by the failure of
his plans to marry
George Sands' niece,
Théodore Rousseau, "Le
Grand Refusé" of the Salon,
decided to isolate himself at
Barbizon. He was accompanied
by his companion Elisa Gros
whose mental fragility would in
time lead to madness. Rousseau
rented a small house (painted in
1907 by Georges Gassies,
Barbizon's first historian) and
turned the barn into a studio.
He spent most of his time in the
majestic forest. From now on he
believed that "he who lives in
silence becomes the center of the
world." He meticulously sought
to present detailed portraits of
the forest in all its intimate
depths.

Concerned for the forest's age-
old virginity, he sought to
have it protected first by Louis-
Philippe, then by
Napoleon III. He therefore
became its first ecologist.

Wolves Gorge in
Fontainebleau Forest
(photo).

Théodore Rousseau: **Entrance to the Forest.**

37

Théodore Rousseau: **Painter Working in the Forest.**

The Louis-Philippe Crossroads
in Fontainebleau Forest
(photo).

Théodore Rousseau: **Fontainebleau Forest, Exit at Sunset** (1849–50).

Illustrated letter by Théodore Rousseau (1865).

Théodore Rousseau: **Road in Fontainebleau Forest, Effects of a Storm** (1860-65).

Théodore Rousseau:
Clearing in the Woods
(1862).

"I listen to the voices of the trees... I discover their passions. The artist's soul must become filled with the infinity of nature." Rousseau, like most of his fellow painters, owed his vocation as a naturalist landscape painter to the 17th century Dutch masters. He may also have inherited their somewhat deifying attitude toward nature, in view of his referral to Fontainebleau as "this ancient place... which we have named Arcadia." Nonetheless, it was through his preoccupation with the variations of

light on the massive forests that he might be considered, along with Corot, as one of the precursors of Impressionism. He affirmed that one must "keep in mind the virgin impression of nature."

In 1885 Rousseau made two versions of **The road out of Fontainebleu forest,** in which he attempted to capture the fluctuations of color, restraining himself to constant complementary retouchings of the canvases.

Georges Gassies: **Millet's Studio and Home** (1863).

Jean-François Millet:
Self Portrait (1845-46).

Jean-François Millet:
Portrait of Catherine Lemaire
(1848-49).

*F*leeing the cholera epidemic in Paris and the aftermath of the 1848 Revolution, Jean-François Millet, his mistress, Catherine Lemaire, and their children went with Charles Jacque to "that place at the edge of the forest whose name ends in zon." Following the example of Rousseau, with whom he became close friends, Millet found a small house on Barbizon's main street and a modest barn to serve as his studio. He renounced the intimidating Parisian world in order to identify with the local farmers who reminded him of the countrymen of his native La Hague, on the north west coast. Cultivating his garden as well as familial bliss, Millet lived and painted according to the biblical rhythms of the cultivation of fields, the felling of trees and the grazing of pastures. He was especially partial to the vast expanses of the plains which evoked childhood memories of the sea's horizon.

Millet's studio at the time of his death in 1875 (photo).

Jean-François Millet and his family in 1854
(from a daguerreotype).

40

Millet's widow in front of their house (photo).

The palette of Jean-François Millet.

Jean-François Millet: **Millet's Garden at Barbizon.**

Jean-François Millet: **Millet's House at Barbizon.**

Gustave Courbet: **Women Winnowing Corn** (1854).

Barbizon painters, including Millet, Courbet and Grigoresco (photo).

Photographic portrait of Courbet.

Photographic portrait of Millet
by Evelyne Cuvelier (1862).

Millet and Courbet had more in common than the physical resemblance that can be noted in the photographs taken of them at Barbizon. Millet, continuing a tradition begun by Louis Le Nain, can be considered as the best painter-anthropologist of disappearing rural life. His **Winnower** (which inspired the young Courbet's **Stonebreakers**) exhibited at the "revolutionary" Salon in 1848, is so precise that, according to the poet Théophile Gautier, the viewer is seized with the desire to sneeze, on seeing the powdery effect of the stirred-up grain.

Courbet, during tumultuous gatherings at the Andler brasserie in 1848 with Daumier, Barye, Decamps, Corot and others, had already launched the aesthetic principles and social foundations of pictorial realism, for which his **Burial at Ornans** was to become the standard.

Many years later Van Gogh would prefer the humble and lyrical paintings of Millet, which he copied lovingly in his own style.

Jean-François Millet: **Shepherd Showing the Way to Travellers.**

Gustave Courbet: **The Stonebreakers.**
Detail (Salon 1849).

Jean-François Millet:
Study for The Winnower.

Jean-François Millet: **The Winnower** (replica of 1848 canvas).

Jean-François Millet: **Midday** (1866).

Vincent Van Gogh: **Midday, after Millet** (1889).

43

44   Jean-François Millet:
     The Angelus (1857-59).

Jean-François Millet: **The Angelus** (1857-59).

Jean-François Millet: **Resting at Midday.** Detail.

The "Belle Marie" who posed in **The Angelus** (photo).

T he world-wide fame today of **The Angelus,** (comparable to that of the **Mona Lisa**), and its numerous reproductions and Surrealist transformations, have so diminished its original force that we forget the humble intentions of its creator. "While working on it I thought of how my grandmother, laboring in the fields, never failed to make us stop to say the angelus for the poor dead when she heard the peal of the church bells."

Using 'Belle Marie' as his model, and inspired by the Chailly plains (of which Ziem has given us a pre-Impressionist view) Millet succeeded in evoking the nostalgia one feels at the moment of dusk. Such a nostalgia can be defined as homesickness for a paradise lost, in which the ringing of a bell recalls the flight of memorable hours.

The Angelus, a novel by René Esse, musical adaptation by Gaston Maquis.

The plains at Chailly-en-Bière (photo).

Jean-François Millet: **Departure for Work** (1863).

Jean-François Millet: **The Church at Chailly.**

The church at Chailly-en-Bière (photo).

Félix Ziem: **The Plains at Chailly, Grey Day** (1860-65).

Jean-François Millet: **The Gleaners** (1857).

Jean-François Millet: **Study for The Gleaners.**

Woman gleaning hay (photo).

In his poem **The Rays and Shadows,** *Victor Hugo* describes the "indistinct hour at the death of day" when the echoes of the angelus are succeeded by the first waves of nightfall. At that hour, exhausted herders linger in the fields, indulgently allowing their flocks to graze an instant longer on the tufts of nourishing earth. "It is thus that the spirit, form, shadow, light and flame/ The urn of the entire world will expand in his soul."

But listen to Millet himself describe his canvases:

"I can clearly see the sun spreading its glory in the distant clouds. I also see the horses laboring on the steamy plains, while in a rocky corner, a man stiff from bending over his work grunts in pain as he tries to straighten himself and catch his breath."

In concluding that art is a combat in which one must be prepared to lose one's skin, Millet's sincerity set an example of a total, almost priest-like commitment, which would later characterize the works of his emulators, particularly Pissarro.

Jean-François Millet: **Twilight** (1858-59).

Jean-François Millet: **Shepherd Watching His Flock.**

Shepherd and flock on the plains at Chailly-en-Bière (photo).

The White Horse Inn's first sign.

Portraits of the proprietors of the White Horse Inn. Painted mural.

White Horse Inn on the main street of Chailly-en-Bière (photo).

Anonymous wall sketches at the White Horse Inn.

Dining room of the White Horse Inn.

In the spring of 1863, Bazille, Monet, Renoir and Sisley ventured into the forest and became pensioners at the White Horse Inn at Chailly-en-Bière. This inn remains unchanged today; its dining-room walls are adorned with sketches and small paintings including portraits of its former proprietors. These works, for the most part anonymous and anecdotal, are admirably done.

It was at the edge of the forest that Diaz, upon meeting Renoir, gave him Rousseau's advice: "Lighten your palette."

In 1865, Monet, in search of a woodland setting for his **Luncheon on the grass,** injured his right leg. He was nursed in a hotel room by his friend Bazille, who at the time was still a medical student. Bazille's pictorial reportage of this incident, **Monet after His Accident,** is full of realism and a comforting humor.

Courtyard and stables at the White Horse Inn today (photo).

Painters under an umbrella.
Wall sketch at the White Horse Inn.

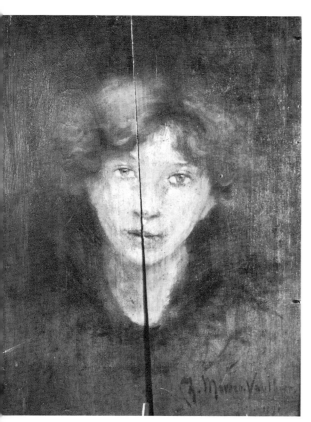

Charles Moreau-Vauthier:
Portrait of a Young Woman.
Wall painting.

Anonymous wall sketches from the White Horse Inn.

Frédéric Bazille: **Monet After His Accident at the Inn in Chailly** (1866).

51

Rosa Bonheur: **Studies of Stags.**

Rosa Bonheur in her studio (photo).

Hunt in Fontainebleau forest (photo).

Antoine-Louis Barye:
Two Panthers in the Dunes at Fontainebleau.

Gustave Courbet:
Hunted Deer, Spring.

Alfred Sisley: **Village Street in Marlotte** (1866).

Wildlife painters also found an appropriate milieu in the forest where hunts had taken place since the time of King François I. Like Courbet, the wildlife painters depicted the nobility of the deer and stags.

In January 1875, a stag hunted down by dogs took refuge in the garden bordering Millet's house. Millet, who was dying, thought he heard the announcement of his own end in the cries of the stag.

Barye, residing in Barbizon, purposely chose to live in the forest because it was inhabited by the same wild animals he had studied, long before Douanier Rousseau, at the Jardin des Plantes.

Rosa Bonheur installed herself in a cottage at By, near Fontainebleau, which she equipped with a small menagerie.

In the nearby village of Marlotte, an entire colony of artists including Alfred Sisley and Auguste Renoir, was established. In 1866 Renoir created **Mother Anthony's Inn,** his first large composition. On the wall, in the background of this painting, is a portrait of de Murger, who was the author of **Scenes from a Bohemian Life,** and the 'discoverer' of Marlotte. Seated around the table are the bearded Monet and Sisley with the artist Jules Lecœur in the middle. They are waited on by Nana, the daughter of the innkeeper whose black-kerchiefed head is visible in the background. It was at this inn that Zola later wrote **L'Assommoir (The Dram-Shop).**

Auguste Renoir: **Mother Anthony's Inn, Marlotte** (1866).

Claude Monet: **Study for Luncheon on the Grass** (1866).

Gustave Courbet: **Hunt Picnic.**

Picnic in the forest during the Second Empire (photo).

Paul Cézanne: **Snow's Effects, Fontainebleau** (c. 1879–80).

Claude Monet: **The Road to Chailly, Fontainebleau Forest** (c. 1865).

Fontainebleau under snow (photo).

Tree-lined road in Fontainebleau (photo).

These celebrated locations were eventually penetrated by the radiant light of the Impressionists. From 1865 on, at the gates of Chailly-en-Bière, Claude Monet widened a gap in the somber woods of Fontainebleau and announced the dawning of a new development in painting. Wanting to challenge Manet, whose **Déjeuner sur l'herbe (Luncheon on the Grass)** had caused a scandal at the Salon of 1863, Monet began a series of paintings of bourgeois picnics. He took the advice of Courbet (who is seated at the center of Monet's painting) and pressed his friends into serving as models. He faithfully reproduced the play of light upon the leaves, the tree trunks, the table cloth and the clothing of the picnickers.

Much later, Cézanne, an enthusiastic admirer of Fontainebleau, used photography to accentuate the structural and somber effects of trees in a winter light which seeps onto the melting snow.

55

2
HONFLEUR
The Pursuit of Light

Michel Lévy: **Eugène Boudin Painting Cows in a Meadow Near Deauville.**

"I LIKE THE CLOUDS... THE passing clouds... yonder... yonder... marvelous clouds," says Baudelaire's alter-ego, the dreamy *Stranger*. This languid dream would take form in Eugène Boudin's heavenly pastels. Enraptured by Boudin's studies of an ever-changing sky, the poet of *Flowers of Evil* predicted in his *Salon of 1859* that "Boudin will, without a doubt, eventually disclose to us the prodigious magic of water and air."

In designating himself herald of the 'King of the heavens'—as Corot called Boudin—Baudelaire also revealed a kingdom where 'knights of the palette' arrived from England, Holland, Paris and Barbizon. They were armed only with paint-brushes, and their mission was to convey the silvery waters of the rivers and fluid richness of the atmosphere.

The Grace Coast is situated on the Seine's sparkling estuary, "a watery landscape set ablaze by the sky's burning rays." For more than four centuries the inhabitants of Normandy, in traditional headdress and flushed with gratitude, gave thanks to the Virgin Mary for the safe homecoming of their schooners. Escorted by screaming sea gulls, these ships could be seen from the cliffs. They were making their valiant

Eugène Boudin: **White Clouds, Blue Sky** (Study of sky c. 1859).

57

return from Louisiana and Antilles, from Newfoundland and Quebec. Their port of entry was Honfleur, the jewel of the Normandy coast, like a black fleur-de-lis against the green fields and azure skies charged with mercury clouds.

Honfleur would also become the new base for the precursors of Impressionism. Falling under the spell of its luminosity and studying the lessons of Eugène Boudin, they were forever searching for the magical effects of the sun on the sea, where sailboats from Le Havre and Trouville pecked away like giant albatross. These pioneers of an ethereal style of painting scoured the hills and valleys of the Normandy countryside. They contemplated its skies where cumulous clouds appeared endlessly, as if herded by some celestial shepherd; and through this they recognized Boudin as the incomparable master of light.

So it is not surprising that Baudelaire was filled with wonder at "these studies, so rapidly and accurately sketched, of the most inconstant and elusive forms and colors—such as waves and clouds—always bearing the date, hour and wind in the margins, for example: October 8th, noon, northwest wind... All of these clouds in fantastic and luminous forms, these chaotic shadows, this green and rose vastness... go to my head like an intoxicating drink or the eloquence of opium."

1859 was a year of grace for Boudin, when this native of Honfleur—son of a steamer boatswain—decided to "swim in the full sky, to reach the tenderness of the clouds... to make the heavens explode." He now regretted those years spent, "making the light so poor, so sad." Boudin was encouraged by the admiration of Baudelaire, Monet and Courbet. It was Courbet who told him: "Name of God, you are a seraphim; you are the only one who understands the sky!"

"My Destiny as a Painter Was Opened Up"

At the end of his life, Claude Monet admitted that he owed his vocation as an artist to Boudin, who had discovered his *charges au crayon*—amusing caricatures of Le Havre's citizens—at a frame dealer's shop. "At his insistence I agreed to go and work with him out-of-doors; I bought a box of paints and we departed for Rouelle, without much conviction on my part. Boudin set up his easel and began working; I watched him with some apprehension. I watched him attentively, and then suddenly, as if a veil had been torn away, I understood. I knew what painting could be. Simply by the example of that artist, engrossed in his art and independence, my destiny as a painter was opened up." The words "opened up" and "torn away" from that confession evoke the window whose curtains Boudin opened wide onto the sea and airy spaces.

Monet wrote to Boudin from Paris on June 3, 1859, commenting on the paintings that were being exhibited at the *Salon* and saying that "marine paintings are completely missing" and that this was Boudin's chance, that marine paintings could be "a road that should take you far." Meanwhile Courbet visited Boudin in June and encouraged him to be bolder. "I shall try some broad paintings, things on a larger scale. At last we are entering into a new art. And so, be brave!", Boudin jotted down in his notebook.

It was Boudin who introduced Courbet to Mother Toutain's farm at Saint-Siméon. There they delighted in dining on shrimps and mussels and her specialty *matelote à la marinière,* a mouth-watering dish that would inspire the painter André Gill to produce a sign in its honor.

Two years before his death, at Deauville in 1896, Boudin wrote about the early days at the Saint-Siméon farm: "Oh Saint-Siméon, what a wonderful legend could be written about that inn!" Evoking his vivid memories, he recounted the joyous festivities, such as the rousing games of skittles with the artist Diaz, "who could hurl a ball with an energetic arm and nimbly knock you down... I visited and traveled all over my little town. Certainly there were years when I was poor, but those were youthful years when hope took the place of money. One had visions of a better future..."

The Saint-Siméon farm was an unforgettable link between the Grace Coast and the haven at Honfleur, where sea, sky and earth often seemed to fuse. The farm, surrounded by apple trees and hawthorne hedges, was situated on a hillside overlooking the sea. One can imagine Mother Toutain, her servant Rose and her daughter "sweet Marie", dressed in full petticoats and traditional cotton bonnets, swiftly descending the steep incline which led directly to the beach, their skirts billowing out and tossing them about like a commotion of bells.

Artists from all over gathered in this modest yet fertile meeting place under the apple trees. They were fascinated by the sunbeams dancing on the fluttering sails and the light sparkling on the waves. A new type of painting was launched, like a skiff heading toward the open sea. Escaping from the clinging shores of Barbizon, it left in its wake a long flotilla of Impressionist, Pointilist and Fauvist canvases.

The Saint-Siméon farm was more than just a casual meeting place for artists. In fact, one can justifiably speak of a "Free School of Saint-Siméon." The exposure to healthy competition and the necessity for self-discipline ensured that a good many artists were actually more successful in their seaside efforts than they had been within the large Paris studios.

Among the artists who spent time at Saint-Siméon, before it became famous, were Isabey, Corot, Boudin, Jongkind, Troyon, Harpignies, Daubigny, Armand Gautier, Diaz, Cals, Monet and Bazille. But three artists in particular, Boudin, Jongkind and Monet were mutually influential and generous.

What was it that made this farm the birthplace of so many works that fell between the Realism of Barbizon and the more allusive Impressionism developed on the banks of the Seine?

There were many determining factors. Its geographical location was exceptional; it was located at the mouth of the Seine facing England, where Constable, Turner and Bonington had developed their fresh water-colorist conceptions of the Anglo-Normandy landscape. A translucent microclimate, always hesitating between rain or shine, necessitated a constant suppleness on the part of the painters who had to execute their works rapidly. Then there was the rural and Norman opportunism of the Toutains and the potential clientèle of shipowners and wealthy tradesmen from the expanding transatlantic port of Honfleur. Visitors also came from the artistic and rich seaport of Rouen. Finally there were the snobbish summer visitors who vacationed at the distinguised beaches at Trouville and Deauville, whose rising vogue followed that of Dieppe, the respectable doyen of French seaside resorts. Dieppe's aristocratic and wealthy vacationers were flattered in portraits by Eugène Isabey, long before Corot, Courbet or Boudin.

The seasonal fashion of sea bathing and beach promenades originated in England and had been inaugurated in France at Dieppe (the nearest beach to Paris) by Queen Hortense, accompanied by Jean-Baptiste Isabey, Napoleon III's portraitist. Queen Hortense's cherished, illegitimate son, the Duke of Morny, was responsible for the installation and opening of the resort at Deauville. This resort rivalled the beach at Trouville which had become particularly prosperous after the construction in 1853 of a railway which transported pale Parisians as far as sunny Rouen.

Eugène Isabey inherited from his father a happy and altruistic nature, friends in high places, and a consummate skill in watercoloring. Scouring the Normandy countryside and coastline in pursuit of views and seascapes, Isabey ended up at Le Havre where he picked out the promising works of Eugène Boudin (exhibited in Boudin's stationery shop). In that same year, 1844, he traveled to Holland and noted the talent of the Dutch painter Johan Barthold Jongkind and urged him to go to Paris and later, to Normandy.

Elective Affinities, Reflexive Waves

In September 1864 Claude Monet, battling with debts, was nevertheless in good spirits when he wrote to his friend Bazille: "We are at Honfleur in large numbers… we have a very agreeable little circle. Jongkind and Boudin are here, we get along wonderfully and won't ever leave each other… there is so much to learn in such company… We sometimes go to Trouville, it's superb. I've promised myself to return there and to go to Etretat as well." Besides these three friends, whose equal ambition inspired a friendly competition, there were also Corot, Daubigny, Troyon, Harpignies, Français, Diaz, Lebourg and Cals staying at Mother Toutain's farm. Art was spreading by elective affinities and reflexive waves.

"One thing which strikes me," wrote Edmund de Goncourt in his journal of June 1882, "is the extent of Jongkind's influence. Any landscape which is of value today descends from his work, borrowing his skies, atmosphere and earth."

Eugène Boudin and Claude Monet have certainly acknowledged their debt of 'reconnaissance' to this Dutchman, who in turn described Eugène Isabey as "my master of painting." Boudin made his acknowledgement in terms full of imagery. "Jongkind began to make us swallow a kind of painting whose tough peel conceals a more delicious fruit. I profited by entering the door that he has forced open." Monet, who met Jongkind at the end of September 1862 (in a meadow, where he was wrestling with a capricious cow), was immediately adopted by him. Monet later confirmed that "complementing the teaching that I received from Boudin, Jongkind was from that moment my true master. I owe the definitive education of my eye to him." There was a reciprocity between these artists which is worth considering; we should realize that masters receive from their students insights that enable them to understand their own work better. This give and take was evident in the work of Jongkind, Boudin and Monet.

There is no doubt that aside from the mutual indebtedness of these three artists and that of their contemporaries and followers, all of them owed their animated approach to painting to the meetings and confrontations at the Saint-Siméon farm. The Grace Coast preceded the Seine and its tributaries, Brittany and Provence, as an area that offered artists the chance to live and work together and to express a newborn hope in painting.

What were the innovations these artists made at Honfleur? How do they relate to the discoveries made at Barbizon?

The answers might be found in Marcel Proust's definition of the art of Elstir, a character in *Remembrance of Things Past:* art was "an effort not to reproduce things as we know them to be, but according to the optical illusions of which our first sight of them is composed." This amounts to an empirical effort, born from the conviction (progressively dismantled until the blossoming of Impressionism) that painting should be more immediate and sensory, and less the "mental thing" claimed by Leonardo da Vinci. The Saint-Siméon painters realized that it is the visual experience of landscape which is best conveyed: its depths lodge on the surface, its beauty is revealed by appearances.

"How is it that you don't know the famous painter Elstir?" Saint-Loup asked the narrator of *Within a Budding Grove* at the restaurant at Rivebelle, a beach resort that Proust modeled on Trouville, Cabourg and Honfleur. "Famous," he elaborated, "Elstir wasn't quite what the patron of the restaurant claimed, although in a few years he was to reach the height of his fame. However, he was the first to frequent the restaurant when it was only a sort of farm, and he brought a whole colony of artists there…"

Elstir was, to a large extent, a combination of the personalities of Boudin and Monet. It is fascinating to pick out their influence in Proust's writings—especially in his completely Impressionistic descriptions of the region's landscape and sea shore. Some of his passages are analogous to Monet's paintings—like the following: "I continued as far as the embankment which mounts steeply towards the fields, decorated here and there by a few lost poppies and lazy blueberries straggling behind… isolated houses already announced the approach of a village… the immense expanses where wheat surges, fleeced by clouds and the sight of a lonely poppy heaving at the end of its stem, a red flame lashing in the wind above its black lifeline… making my heart beat, like a voyager who sees a grounded boat being repaired, and who cries, even before he sees it: The Sea!"

Rimbaud too rejoiced in the fleeting but decisive visions of the Grace Coast painters in his poem on eternity, written in 1872:

It has been found   It is the sea going
What?—Eternity   with the sun.

There was nothing more attractive for these artists than the secret but impassioned interactions of sun and sea. Nothing was more durable than the ephemeral reconciliations between light and shadow.

HOTEL-RESTAURANT SAINT-SIMÉON — Honfleur

Louis-Alexandre Dubourg: **Norman Woman at her Window**
(Drawing from an unpublished sketch book).

The Saint-Siméon Farm (postcard).

Norman Woman circa 1859. (Boudin legacy).

C orot the Itinerant, always interested in harmonious landscapes, visited Normandy in 1829 "to see a small town called Trouville which is teeming with charming motifs." Having discovered the charms of Honfleur he would later return to paint the **Toutain Farm.** Trouville had since become a society beach, and artists eager for solitude soon abandoned it in favor of Honfleur. The farm at Saint-Siméon was not yet the famous hotel-restaurant that it would become by the end of the century.

In 1903 a disappointed Picasso wrote: "it was once a farm surrounded by apple trees planted in green fields with a view of the sea. Boudin, Corot, Daubigny, Monet and Jongkind all went there. Now there is nothing left of that glorious past…"

Located at the edge of Honfleur on the isolated site of a former home for lepers, the farm, dedicated to the medieval Saint-Siméon, resembles those painted earlier by Monet. Run by a Norman couple, the Toutains, it was known for its rustic, welcome atmosphere and its copious table at which visitors often remained from noon until evening.

One can recognize Mother Toutain's features in Boudin's Portrait of **A Norman Woman** and in the unusual sketches by Dubourg, one of her most frequent guests.

Louis-Alexandre Dubourg: **Cat**
(Drawing from an unpublished sketchbook).

Camille Corot: **The Toutain Farm at Honfleur.**

Adolphe-Félix Cals: **Honfleur Woman Unravelling Yarn** (1877).

Claude Monet: **Farmyard in Normandy** (c. 1863).

Louis-Alexandre Dubourg: **Farmyard, or Tables at Saint-Siméon.**

Louis-Alexandre Dubourg: **Lunch at the Saint-Siméon Farm.**

Louis-Alexandre Dubourg:
Dog and Her Puppies
(Drawing from an unpublished sketch book).

Gathered at the large wooden tables set in a field overlooking the beach, the artists toasted the health of the smocked farmers and Mother Toutain. Louis-Alexandre Dubourg conveys the convivial ambiance that reigned over these occasions in his **Tables at Saint-Siméon.**

Boudin was a frequent visitor and often brought his friends, among them Courbet, who claimed that the cider was only good for washing his hands, but who nevertheless dozed off after a few drinks from "Father Toutain's little cask." Boudin's lively sketch of a **Group of Painters at the Saint-Siméon Farm,** captured Jongkind, Emile Van Marcke, Claude Monet (raising his glass) and 'old' Jean Achard, enjoying the hospitality of the Toutain farm.

Eugène Boudin: **Drinkers at Saint-Siméon** (c. 1869).

André Gill: **Sign for the Saint-Siméon Farm.**

Engraving after André Gill's sign.

Eugène Boudin: **Group of Painters at the Saint-Siméon Farm**
(Left to right: Jongkind, Emile Van Marcke, Claude Monet and père Achard).

The Saint-Siméon farm (photograph).

S ated with shrimps and sole, leg of lamb, partridge and apples (see Boudin's still life), inebriated by the burning "flips" made by Father Toutain from coffee and calvados, the artists retired to their rooms. There they left traces of their exaltation on walls and doors—drawings, caricatures and frescoes in charcoal, chalk or paint, which the owner quickly whitewashed. Français and Boudin also made several seascapes in oil.

In 1860, René Ménard and Stéphane Baron executed a **Last Judgement,** in the style of Michelangelo, in one of the ground floor rooms. Called the "Chamber of Hell," the room was where the Toutain's son died during a spell of delirium tremens, "terrified by the twitching burning men" painted on the walls.

Paul Huet: **Apple Trees on the Grace Coast** (1829).

Adolphe-Félix Cals: **Lunch at Honfleur** (1875).

Farm in Normandy (photo).

Eugène Boudin: **The Saint-Siméon Farm** (sketch c. 1859).

Home distiller at Saint-Siméon (photo).

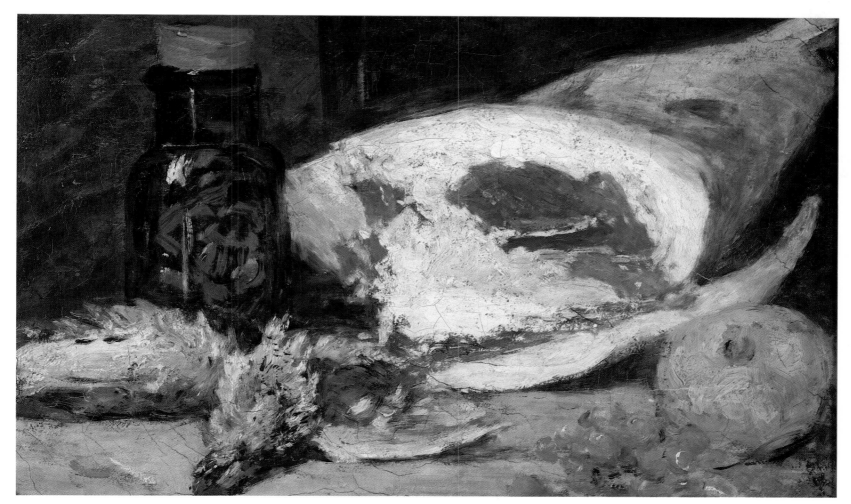

Eugène Boudin: **Still Life with a Leg of Lamb** (c. 1859).

Notre-Dame de Grâce Chapel at Honfleur (photo).

Louis-Alexandre Dubourg: **Notre-Dame de Grâce Chapel.**

Johan Barthold Jongkind: **Grâce Chapel, Honfleur** (September 14, 1864).

The draughtsmen, watercolorists, painters and engravers had to cross only a few yards to reach the magnificent chapel of Notre Dame de Grâce. Rebuilt in the 18th century, a haven of model sailing ships offered by sailors in recognition of her protection, the chapel also became a favorite spot for pictorial pilgrimages.

In 1864, Johan Barthold Jongkind portrayed this chapel in one of his new watercolors, which he dedicated to Madame Fesser, his oracle. The watercolor would later be greatly admired by the Impressionists. In the meantime, the young Monet tried his own version of the same subject, and in it we can see traces of the development of his personal style. Dubourg also depicted the chapel, but his version is marked by Romanticism.

Deeply sensitive to the Norman countryside, Monet composed many poetic canvases, including several snow scenes, during the winter of 1866-67. In shattering cold, equipped with a foot-warmer, three sweaters and thick gloves, Monet freezes the wintry silence of a lone magpie perched on a fence.

Claude Monet: **Notre-Dame de Grâce Chapel** (1864).

Claude Monet: **The Magpie** (1867).

Claude Monet: **A Cart on a Snow Covered Road Near Honfleur** (1867).

Heather bordered path in Honfleur (photo).

69

Gustave Courbet: **The Mouth of the Seine** (c. 1841).

Calvary at Notre-Dame de Grâce plateau (photo).

The Grace Coast (photo).

Camille Corot: **Calvary of Grace Coast at Honfleur** (c. 1830).

Georges Braque: **Grace Coast at Honfleur** (1905).

Henri–Charles Manguin: **Honfleur, View of the Grace Coast** (1910).

"**A**rriving at the summit of the Grace Coast by way of a sinuous path, one discovers on the horizon the infinite meeting of sea and the eye. In the distance, a boat gliding like a large swan is dissolved in the fog. The platform of the coast is carpeted with a thick green lawn and everything is covered with large trees... At a higher point is a large Crucifix which can be seen from far off at sea." That description by Alphonse Karr, who lived in Honfleur around 1835, remains as topical as the serene visions painted between 1830-1910 by artists such as Corot, Courbet, Braque Manguin and Vallotton.

Many other painters were also impressed by that estuary which is both the Seine and the sea; the sea always refreshed by the tides and winds, like the foliage which is ever renewed. It was this constant renewal of greenery that prompted Alphonse Allais, the famous Honfleur humorist, to found the S.P.V. (Society for the Protection of Vegetation), whose responsibility was to "place mattresses under the trees in order to cushion the falling leaves."

The composer Erik Satie, another native of Honfleur, put that same spirit into music in his **Secular and Instantaneous Hours.**

Félix Vallotton: **Honfleur and the Seine Estuary, Grey Evening** (1910).

The old dock at Honfleur (photo).

Gustave Courbet: **Portrait of Baudelaire** (1845–1850).

Rue de la Bavolle, Honfleur (photo).

L ooking at Courbet's portrait of Baudelaire, one is tempted to ask which poem he had in mind. Perhaps he was thinking of these phrases: "Free man, you will always cherish the sea/ Within the infinite unfurling of its swell/ And your spirit is still a bitter chasm."

Baudelaire often went down to the port by way of the **Rue de la Bavolle.** Leaving the mysterious shadows cast by the medieval buildings, like the man in Monet's painting, he headed towards the sea that was reflected in the brightness of the blue sky.

Claude Monet: **Rue de la Bavolle, Honfleur** (c. 1866).

Although attributed to Claude Monet by his son, this **Steeple of Sainte-Catherine** *was probably done by Boudin, who may have given it to Monet. Boudin clearly conveys the shaky and hatched impression given by the church's 15th century tower. This wooden tiled tower also attracted the attention of Jongkind. His eye was taken by the vibrant geometry of the half-timbered houses resting on lopsided foundations worn away by rain and the sea. One can still see today this same steeple pointing its finger at the sky.*

Sainte-Catherine. Attributed to Claude Monet (c. 1867).

Sainte-Catherine, Honfleur (photo).

Johan Barthold Jongkind: **Sainte-Catherine, Honfleur** (1864).

Johan Barthold Jongkind: **Street in Honfleur** (1863).

Louis-Alexandre Dubourg: **Bathers at Honfleur.**

Bathing costumes (from the magazine **Illustrated Fashions,** 1878).

Honfleur, although primarily a fishing and transit port, followed the example of Trouville and Deauville in renovating its bathing spots on the Grace Coast. Dubourg painted the carefree, yet cautious bathers on these new beaches. Perhaps that is Mother Toutain pacing the beach in search of shells, while fishing boats enter the estuary in the background.

Monet depicted the **Lighthouse at Honfleur,** *painting the rippling waves with "tiny curling brushstokes."*

The Divisionist, Seurat, was in turn fascinated by the Channel's "indefinable" greys. In 1885 he took great pains to capture the greys of the Hospice lighthouse and port. His geometric combinations of the hulls, funnels and masts of the steamers enhance the phantomlike character of the solitary quays.

Fisherman on the beach at Honfleur (photo).

Louis-Alexandre Dubourg: **Beach at Honfleur.**

Lighthouse at Honfleur (photo).

The jetty at Honfleur (photo).

Claude Monet: **Lighthouse at Honfleur** (1864).

Georges Seurat: **La Maria, Honfleur** (1866).

Louis-Alexandre Dubourg: **Jetty at Honfleur** (1879).

Louis-Alexandre Dubourg:
Sketch of Sailboats.

Exit from the port of Honfleur (photo).

T*he call of the sea and the enchantment of the future were themes that inspired these painters. The piers, bustling with the activity of ships casting off and spectators waving handkerchiefs and parasols, caught the attention of Dubourg and Jongkind. This atmosphere captivated the Saint-Siméon artists whose ambition was to sail toward the light. Breaking away from the instantaneous techniques of watercolor, Jongkind used oils to convey these fugitive illusions and great hopes.*

Johan Barthold Jongkind:
Entrance to the Port of Honfleur (1866).

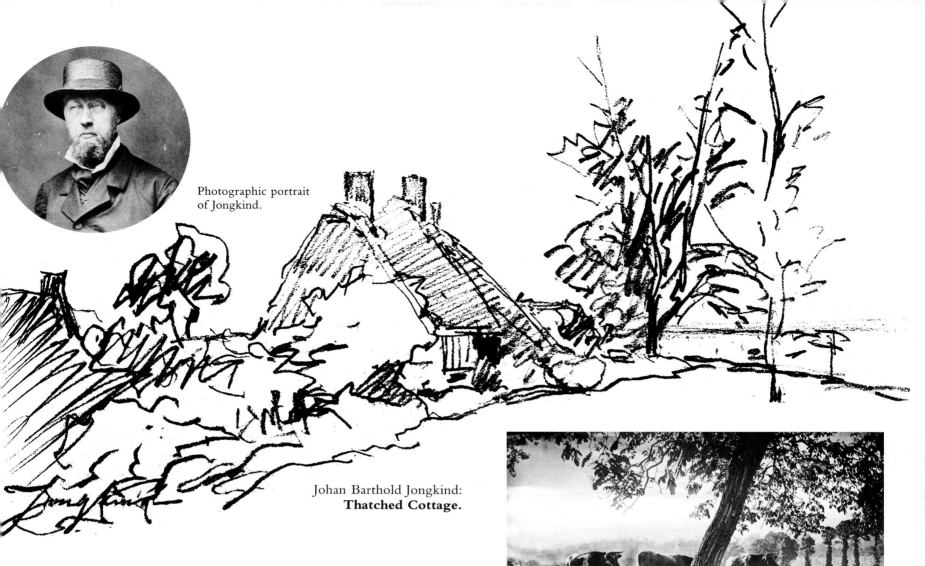

Photographic portrait of Jongkind.

Johan Barthold Jongkind:
Thatched Cottage.

Robert Demachy: **Cows in Normandy** (photo).

Jongkind and Boudin strove for the restoration of life, whether in the rhythms of a simple graphite sketch of an old thatched cottage, or in an oil sketch of the invading fog. In the same way, Robert Demachy tried with pictorial photography to seize upon the oblique radiance of the sun which almost seems to be prodding the sun-dappled cows forward into the retreating shadows.

Eugène Boudin:
Cows Near the Sea
(c. 1890-97).

Eugène Boudin painting
on the boardwalk at Deauville (photo).

Eugène Boudin: **Women and Children in front of the Casino at Trouville** (c. 1874).

The beach at Trouville (photo).

Women and children
on the beach at Trouville (photo).

Eugène Boudin: **Beach at Trouville, The Conversation** (1876).

"They like my little women on the beach; some claim that there is something here worth exploiting," Boudin wrote to one of his friends in February 1863. That "something worth exploiting," revealed to Boudin by Eugène Isabey, were the beaches at Trouville and Deauville. The 'King of the Skies' became the master of beaches. Crinolines, flowered hats and veils, shawls, black hats and yellow boaters, rainbow colored tents and umbrellas were all caught by Boudin's paintbrush. Boudin worked on location, asserting that "everything painted directly on the spot always has a strength, a power, a vividness of touch that one doesn't find in the studio." This was a lesson in spontaneity to which Monet instinctively responded.

Claude Monet: **Camille Monet and Her Cousin on the Beach at Trouville** (1870).

Eugène Boudin: **Beach at Trouville** (1863).

View of a beach (photo).

"What a masquerade? You have to be a genius to give a good account of that band of idle show-offs," complained Boudin. However, Boudin was in fact much more patient with his subjects than his tirade shows. In fact he once defended his interest in painting people on the beaches: "The peasants have their painters... that is fine, but, those middle-class people who stroll on the jetty at sunset, don't they also have the right to be portrayed, to be brought to our attention. After all, they are often resting after work, these people who leave their offices and cubbyholes. If there are a few parasites among them, there are also people who have done their work."

Boudin was conscious of Corot's grace, Daubigny's ease, Jongkind's fluidity and Courbet's daring and wanted to "to do away with the timidity that is still noticeable in my painting." Baudelaire had told him that "the study of the beautiful is like a duel where the artist cries out with fear before being defeated." Boudin was not yet defeated by pure beauty. Undaunted by the "little dolls" on the beach, Boudin blended them all with the elements—the dry and damp sands and the air saturated with sea spray. He turned his models into vibrating plays of light and colors.

Eugène Boudin: **Woman with a Parasol on the Beach at Trouville** (c. 1880).

ugène Boudin: **Beach at Trouville** (1863).

Bathing time at Trouville (photo).

Casino terrace at Etretat (photo).

83

Eugène Isabey: **The Rocks at Etretat** (1857).

The beach at Etretat (photo).

Following in Delacroix's more or less hardy footsteps, Eugène Isabey and Jongkind were among the first painters at Etretat to survey its pebbly beach and climb its ruined cliffs. Courbet, while staying at the house of an artist friend, depicted its ramparts, divided between the earth and the sea. Guy de Maupassant met him there and described him—face glued to the window, fascinated by a storm, plastering layers of paint onto his canvas with a kitchen knife. Despite its earthy solidity, Courbet's **Cliffs at Etretat after a storm** shows the influence of the Saint-Siméon painters in the subtle portrayal of the sea and sky.

Gustave Courbet: **Cliffs at Etretat After a Storm** (1869).

The cliffs at Etretat (photo).

In his novel **Pierre and Jean,** *Guy de Maupassant's description of the cliffs, was no doubt inspired by Monet's canvas: "A large triangle of silver blue water is framed by the green coast... the rocks resemble the ruins of a lost city which looked out over the sea in bygone days." Invited by Courbet to dine with Alexandre Dumas at the Belle-Ernestine Inn, Monet returned more than once to conquer the demolished slopes. These cliffs also attracted Corot, Boudin, Degas, and Renoir.*

Eugène Boudin: **Cliffs at Etretat** (c. 1890–94).

Claude Monet: **Etretat, Rough Sea** (1883).

Gustave Courbet: **Sunset Over the Estuary.**

Le Havre.
Boats returning from Trou
(photo).

Edouard Manet: **Boats at Sunset** (1872–73).

Port of Le Havre (photo).

Eugène Boudin: **Twilight Over the Commercial Dock at Le Havre** (1892-94).

Charles-François Daubigny: **Sunset.**

Nothing was more tempting to the painters who leaned towards Impressionism than the "landscape of the sea" at twilight. It was those few moments that turned them into children of the night, defiantly arresting the sun's farewell. Having flattered the waves all day long, it set without fail, leaving scarlet traces on the sea, while tardy tugboats and steamers hastened towards the port.

Even Courbet and Daubigny, men of the soil, were drawn by this fabulous coupling of water and fire. Monet and Boudin, touched by the nostalgia of the docks at Le Havre, evoked the yearning of anchored vessels reminiscing about their last crossings.

In the meantime, Manet, who was at Boulogne, paid his own homage in the simplicity of **Boats at Sunset.**

Claude Monet went to stay with his aunt in Sainte-Adresse for the summer of 1867. There he depicted his father seated in the sunny, floral and windy domestic atmosphere of the **Terrace at Ste. Adresse.** This painting, which he had clearly mastered from an overhead perspective, was an immediate success. "They are charmed by me and they admire every brushstroke," he wrote to his friend Bazille, proud of his own bravado. And it was indeed a triumphant feat.

In 1870 Monet voyaged to London where he discovered the fourth visionary dimension which Turner had conferred upon his paintings. Structural forms now gave way to the primacy of the pictorial materials, like the sun giving way to the fog. Putting the lessons that he had learned from Turner into practice, Monet painted **Impression. Sun Rising** from his window overlooking the port at Le Havre. The painting was shown at the first independent exhibition of the future 'Impressionists' in 1874. Poking fun at this painting, the critic Louis Leroi was unknowingly responsible for christening this group of artists the "Impressionists."

Claude Monet: **Terrace at Ste-Adresse** (1867).

Claude Monet: **Impression, Sunrise** (1872).

The beach at Ste-Adresse (photo).

The outer harbor at Le Havre (photo).

Edouard Manet:
Portrait of Monet (1874).

Raoul Dufy: **Beach of the Casino Marie-Christine at Sainte-Adresse** (1904).

"Impressionist on the beach"
(postcard of Marquet painting).

Albert Marquet: **The Beach at Ste-Adresse** (1906).

Albert Marquet: **Outer Harbor at Le Havre, Pilot's Cove.**

T*he painters attempted to portray the world as it appeared to them on first sight. They saw midday at their windows, the sun within their reach, and passers-by in their image.*
"Around 1905-06," explained Raoul Dufy, "I painted on the beach at Sainte-Adresse. Up until that time I had painted beaches in the Impressionist style and hadn't yet reached the saturation point. I understood that by copying nature exactly in this manner, I would be led to infinity—in all its complexities and most minute details. I remained outside of the canvas. One day, having reached a standstill and unable to endure it any longer, I began to look at my paint tubes. How can I convey my reality, that is, not what I see but what exists for me? The whole problem was there! And so I began to draw and to choose what I wanted from nature."

A native of Le Havre, Dufy soon forgot Boudin and became a Fauve, like his friend Albert Marquet, who had already taken that road. Therefore, the photographer who caught Marquet at work on the beach was mistaken in calling him an Impressionist. Marquet had in fact already turned toward a new style of color simplification, suggesting it in smooth pools and schematized forms, reducing and outlining them.

Le Havre: pilot's cove and breakwater (photo).

3
THE SEINE
AND ITS TRIBUTARIES
Fine Sundays on the Waterfront

THE SKY ALL PALE, THE TREES
so frail
Seem to smile at our pastel wear,
Floating lightly on the summer air,
With nonchalance, like the wings of quail.

These light, almost hesitant lines from Verlaine's *Fêtes Galantes* were published in 1869, the same year that Renoir and Monet, working together, performed the miracle of making light walk on water. They marked its approach across *La Grenouillère (The Frog Pond)* and dissolved the courtesans and seducers who frequented this spot. Their choice of subject matter proved that the young school of Impressionism was in keeping with the spirit of the times.

In the same year, Carpeaux created his graceful sculptural group *The Dance* which looms from the façade of the Paris Opera. *The Dance,* which makes an irresistable appeal to the art of movement, was the ultimate celebration of the hedonistic years before the Franco-Prussian War in 1870, and the subsequent fall of the Second Empire.

"A work of art is determined by a combination of the general mood and the moral climate," wrote Hippolyte Taine in 1865, in *Philosophy of Art,* insisting on the decisive role that 'milieu' plays in determining an artist's motivation. Napoleon III sums up this notion more prosaically in his remark to the Empress Eugénie, whose favorite preoccupation was the organization of costume balls and other spectacular events at the Tuileries: "Eugénie, you have but one idea and you are possessed by it!" The Empress's idea was one which took possession not only of the aristocracy and the stuffy bourgeoisie, but also exercised its power over the "lower classes." Let's go out, dance, amuse ourselves! Life will pass by as if in a dream.

People danced everywhere. They waltzed at the Bal Mabille, at the Bal Bullier, in Batignolles and Montmartre. They also waltzed at the barriers, at the gates of Paris and on the banks of the Seine, where *guinguettes* (open-air cafés), pleasure boats and landing piers quickly sprang up.

In 1837, the first railway line was inaugurated in France. The line was created to link Paris with Saint-Germain-en-Laye and its important river port at Pecq. It passed through Clichy (and therefore the artists' quarter at Batignolles), Colombes, Nanterre, Rueil and Chatou. The train's route crisscrossed the Seine and areas which later became popular for Parisian Sunday outings. A number of artists had already fallen under the spell of Bougival, and they began decorating the walls of the local inn, following the practice established at Barbizon by Corot, Anastasi and Français.

Taking the train was an intoxicating experience. Victor Hugo wrote to his wife, "The speed is incredible; the flowers beside the tracks are no longer flowers but splashes of red, or white stripes. What once appeared as separate dots now appear as continuous streaks. Corn fields turn into large yellow webs, the alfalfa becomes long green tresses. Trees dance and become chaotically mingled on the horizon." Hugo's description shows that he was an Impressionist before his time. He was also exaggerating a bit, since the trains only traveled at a speed of 31 miles per hour!

After Courbet and his *Young Women on the banks of the Seine* (exhibited in the Salon of 1857), came Manet and the scandal caused by his famous *Déjeuner sur l'herbe (Luncheon on the Grass)*. The idea for this painting came to him while walking along the banks of the Seine with Antonin Proust: "I am going to do a nude in the transparency of the atmosphere, with people like those over there." Intrigued by the fuss made over Manet's painting and curious about the pleasures reputed to be found at La Grenouillère, Napoleon III decided to see for himself what all this was about... However, no nude women were to be seen—Manet had painted his women in the studio. Nor did Napoleon III realize that this riverside café would serve as a baptismal font for the most beautiful new school of painting ever to bring honor to his country.

The spontaneous emergence of Impressionism on Croissy Island at Bougival, was no mere act of chance; nor was it the result of two geniuses meeting in that popular river area, and discovering that their private research coincided. This movement grew out of the efforts of many individuals who worked together and alone. Despite the fact that it received its name at the time of its first exhibition, its origins go farther back than 1874. Although it may have appeared peculiar and ridiculous to the public, Impressionism in fact came from the convergence of many influences (most of which have been mentioned in Chapters I and 2). The movement corresponded to the growing expectations of a civilization that had actually generated the art. This same civilization reacted first with shock, then with appreciation, and finally (according to Bernard Dorival) with enthusiasm at "the splendor of a name which at first was a form of derision."

What did Monet and Renoir do that was so astonishing? What exactly were the innovations that they had surreptitiously introduced into their twin versions of *La Grenouillère?* Looking at these works today, we must see them through the eyes of the painters' critics and contemporaries.

Renoir and Monet hoped to give an illusion of life by deliberately applying horizontal, juxtaposed strokes in dark and light colors, using a mixture of fine, transparent and blurred pigments. They wanted to depict the world in all its palpitations—in the same way that the shimmering heat creates a mirage in the desert, convincing us that water is nearby. With squinting eyes and eager hands, they strove to give the 'impression' (term already used by Delacroix, Corot and some of the Barbizon and Honfleur painters) of a pulsating universe. Their feverish and sensitive brushes restored the reflections of light to the river's waves, captured the lustrous foliage caressed by the passing breeze, the morning mist or the scorching haze of the afternoon. At La Grenouillère they found all these things, as well as the lively animation of the river people and Sunday afternoon visitors. Radiant young women, in all their finery, awaited the dinghies or sail boats that would carry them off to flirt on the river and lead them to Cythera, the mythical home of Aphrodite, the goddess of Love. This was the island from which the 18th century painter Watteau embarked his nostaglic lovers. As the poet Mallarmé noted, it was important for these artists to "paint not the thing, but the effect that it produces."

A Vibrato of Colored Marks

Renoir and Monet were optimists looking for live sources and were only satisfied when recreating the undulating optical fields of life's uncertain appearances. In their wake came an entourage of artists—Sisley, Caillebotte, Mary Cassatt, Berthe Morisot, Manet, Pissarro, Cézanne, Seurat and Gauguin—who discovered the river and its magic. Like Renoir and Monet, they found that the vibration of color on the water and the river banks depended essentially upon the refraction of light. They had to proceed by allusion and approximation, painting in light, quick strokes to finish their canvases on the spot. In this way they caught nature's most subtle, fleeting reality and the transience of the summer visitors. From now on their painting claimed the right to live freely, graciously and harmoniously. Their works reflected a deep sensuality derived from Rubens, Watteau, Fragonard and Delacroix.

In a gay and green dress ruched and lapped,
One June day when I seemed filled with trouble,
She, smiling, suddenly appeared as if from a bubble,
Which made me marvel and fear no trap.

This "little fairy" that Verlaine balanced on the tip of his goosequill pen resembles the light which the Impressionists spread in tiny brushstrokes. "Since I am impressed, there ought to be many impressions in that" quipped their detractors ironically. Of course there was more to it: "A vibrato of colored marks scattering and dancing, dissolving and blending with formerly distinct elements in an atomic waltz of the atmosphere," as René Huyghe described this movement in *Art and the Soul*. "Impressionism, in perceiving light instead of shapes, preceded modern science in seeing the flow of energy in reality."

What an ambition—to set limits on the intangible and invisible! To portray the least consistent materials: the rippling waters, rolling in the wake of boats; or the young women trembling with excitement as their gallant young men show off their diving, while small children frolic among the wild flowers... what patience was needed to paint the presence and absence of things!

"Anne, sister Anne, do you see anything coming?" children call out from one bridge to another. "I see only the grass becoming greener, the river more rippling and the sun more hazy," the artists might have replied. "And we, we see the skiffs bumping into each other and young men bribing blushing young women" might have been the response of their myopic contemporaries who found this fresh conception of the world incomprehensible. Their judgement of art was based on the flatteringly realist, pompous Neo-classical paintings imposed by the Emperor's Salon and Court.

And yet the new school was inevitable. Indeed, one might ask where else could it have developed other than on the Ile-de-France and the banks of the Seine and its tributaries. And it could have happened at no other time than the years immediately before and after the Franco-Prussian war—a catastrophe that had to be forgotten at all costs.

Everything pointed the way to purely naturalistic, phototropic and euphoric aims, which were sorted out instinctively, but which also would be backed up by the chemist Chevreuls' studies on "the simultaneous contrasts of color." Seurat and Signac sought to apply these discoveries in their efforts to codify the optical laws of Impressionism. The result of their experimentation led to the invention of the pointilist techniques of Divisionism.

An Atmosphere of Harmony

The Impressionists were sensitive to the luminescence of Corot's ponds, the reverberations of Boudin's seascapes, the bustling of Jongkind's harbors, and the misty passages in English landscape (particulary Turner). However, it was Daubigny who must be credited with having introduced them to water. Thanks to Daubigny, the Impressionists dissolved the petrified Realism of the Barbizon painters, while still appreciating their return to the soil and open air. Daubigny's passion for the fluid and marbled beauty of the river Oise soon caught the Impressionist's attention. Monet was particularly intrigued by Daubigny's method of painting from his boat-studio and did likewise at Argenteuil. In 1861, Théophile Gautier wrote of Daubigny, "It is too bad that a landscape painter with such a real, accurate and natural talent, is content with an impression... his landscapes offer only patches of juxtaposed colors."

In 1865, Renoir wrote to Bazille, suggesting that they descend the river Seine by boat in order to join Monet at Le Havre for the regatta: "I am bringing my box of paints to sketch the places that please me... We'll be towed as far as Rouen, and from there we are free do do as we like." Four years later, while Renoir was staying with his mother in Louveciennes, Monet, broke as usual, decided to go to nearby Saint-Michel-de-Bougival. There, both fell under the spell of the floating open-air café, La Grenouillère. This recreation spot was swarming with Sunday athletes from the suburbs of Paris, proud of their striped jerseys and immaculate white tousers, accompanied by hearty young women ready for boating or swimming. Nicknamed the "grenouilles" ("girls of the frog pond"), these women were described by Guy de Maupassant as dolled up in "screaming bad taste." Buxom, rounded and puffed up with pride, they thought only of their success at the Bal des Canotiers (Boatmen's Dance) where Renoir found them.

Not far away, near the Chatou bridge, was the Fournaise restaurant and pier which competed with La Grenouillère. This was one of Renoir's favorite places. "It was a perpetual party; I was always satiated at Fournaises. I found all the superb girls that I could desire. My friends knew that for me, a women is only a pretext for a picture." It was rumored that before his marriage to Alice Charigot, Renoir only made love with "the end of his paintbrush." Meanwhile, underneath the boat house, *père* Fournaise had set aside several rooms for his clients who wanted to quietly enjoy a delicious siesta.

Renoir wanted his canvases to express the joy of life. In the *Boatmen's Lunch* he was able to prolong that delectable moment at the end of a good meal when friends idly take pleasure in each other's company. A quarter of a century later, in this same but now-deserted place, Vlaminck and Derain threw themselves into the rage of Impressionist color that became Fauvism. It is said that they shouted back and forth "I'm painting everything red"—"I'm doing everything blue." Then, at the Levanneur Restaurant, next door to the Fournaise, they worked side by side, competing in furious colors.

Some of Impressionism's most golden moments were spent in the harmonious atmosphere of Argenteuil. Monet was the first to go there, followed by Renoir, Sisley, Caillebotte, and Manet. They renamed this pretty riverside village, home of their water muse, "Argentœil" ("Silver Eye"). Gustave Caillebotte, a wealthy art-lover and a painter in his own right, offered his Impressionist friends the use of his boats. Caillebotte was a vigorous moral and financial supporter of his comrades. Manet also became interested in the sun—drenched regattas admired by his friends and began painting out-of-doors. From 1872 to 1875 the Impressionists' airy, delicately shining canvases rivaled one another in the perfect mastery of contrasting and competing colors. These included works that gave dazzling testimony to an art at its height. Following this period, the various artists dispersed and returned to more personal creations.

So, while Seurat 'pointilized' Asnières and the Island of the Grande Jatte, soon to be joined and imitated by Signac, the masters of Impressionism pursued their own paths. From now on they were confident enough to make greater innovations, each in his own way. Renoir entered into what he called his "Ingresque" phase—referring to his drawing as "sharp lines." Voluptuous bathers soon monopolized his paint brushes—"When I look at a nude I see a myriad of shades." He finally settled in the south of France where the azure Mediterranean invaded his canvases. Sisley became isolated in misery at Moret-sur-Loing and consoled himself on the river banks, sketching his memories of Fontainebleau. Pissarro, always attuned to rising young generations, navigated towards the scintillting Divisionism of Seurat and Signac and headed straight for Rouen.

After stopping at Vétheuil, Monet, of all the Impressionists the most faithful to aquatic inspiration, ended by taking root like an old weeping willow on the shores of his garden pond at Giverny. However, before completely settling down, he visited Rouen and London and discovered Venice. This Italian city, floating on phosphorescent canals, was the subject of many canvases. "These landscapes of water and reflections have become an obsession" he wrote in 1908. An obsession? Perhaps more a vision, one that would accompany him until his death in 1926. This vision continued to flow under the bridges of Paris where his waterlilies blossom even today in the Tuileries Garden.

Charles-François Daubigny:
The Departure.

Giorgione: **Concert Champêtre** (Detail).

Gustave Courbet: **Young Women on Banks of the Seine.**

Marcantonuo Raimondi: **Judgement
of Paris** (Detail) after Raphael.

R ejected as 'indecent' by the Salon of 1863,
Manet's **Déjeuner sur l'herbe
(Luncheon on the grass)** caused a
great scandal at the Salon des Refusés. Although
he may have borrowed the design from Giorgione
and Raphael, the modernity of its execution seems
closer to Courbet's "young women of easy virtue,"
whose lascivious abandon in the open air was
considered unacceptable.

Victorine Meurent sits between two conven-
tionally dressed young men in a disconcertingly
relaxed pose, regarding the spectator
with amusement while her companion rinses herself
in the water. This pictorial provocation became a
moral challenge—leading art toward nature and the
natural.

Bazille had this in mind when he painted
Family Reunion, remembering that he himself
had posed for Monet at a luncheon in the forest.

Cézanne criticized Manet's picnic as lacking "the
thrill which brings divine ecstacy to all the senses,"
and began making objects vibrate in unison with the
Provençal light and the chirping cicadas, in order to
mingle with natures elements.

Édouard Manet: **Le Déjeuner sur l'herbe** (1863).

Paul Cézanne: **Le Déjeuner sur l'herbe** (1873–75).

Frédéric Bazille:
Family Reunion (1867).

99

Pierre-Auguste Renoir: **La Grenouillère** (1869).

La Grenouillère, a famous floating café moored at Bougival, was painted by both Monet and Renoir. Working together, they applied for the first time the large dabs of juxtaposed and shimmering paint that became the trademark of Impressionism.

In his short story **Paul's Wife,** Guy de Maupassant described La Grenouillère: *"An immense raft, covered in tarpaulin and supported by wooden columns, is linked to the charming Croissy island by two footbridges. One of these leads into the middle of that aquatic establishment, while the other leads to a tiny islet with a tree which has been nicknamed the 'Flower Pot', and from there to the bathing office."*

It was a paradise for athletes, bathers and boatsmen escorting their *"grenouilles"* (young women of the frog pond). It was also, according to de Maupassant, the haunt of an entire world of *"journalists, show-offs, young men with private incomes, scoundrels, degenerates, and rogues."* Renoir, the Watteau of the 19th century, would embark them all for the mythical island of Cythera.

Oreste Cortazzo:
La Grenouillère.
Woodcut illustration for
Guy de Maupassant's *Yvette*.

La Grenouillère at Chatou (photo).

Edouard Riou:
**Paris in the Country
or La Grenouillère.**

La Grenouillère
at Chatou (photo).

"The customers seated at the tables swallow red, white, yellow and green liquids… a swimmer appears on the roof each second and jumps into the water, splashing those nearby who respond with wild cries." Such is the description given by Maupassant in his novel **Yvette.** Finding La Grenouillère a bit too wild and dissolute, neither Renoir nor Monet remained there for long. Renoir went to stay with his parents at Louveciennes, while Monet, using the last of his money, rented a small house at nearby Bougival. In a letter to Bazille, Renoir wrote, "We might not eat everyday, but I'm content because Monet is great company for painting." The several weeks that these two artists shared at La Grenouillère that summer, marked the beginning of a friendship and an artistic partnership that lasted for many years to come. Their shared explorations produced some of the most important innovations arising from Impressionism.

Guillaume Apollinaire composed the following poem in 1912, after passing some time at La Grenouillère: "From the island's shores one sees the empty canoes bumping one another, and now
neither Sunday nor the days of the week
Neither the painters nor Maupassant walk there
in shirtsleeves accompanied by plump women as silly as cabbages.
Little boats you make me so sad
From the island's shores."

Ferdinand Lunel: **La Grenouillère.**

Paul Destez: **Thursday Evening Dance at La Grenouillère.**

Claude Monet: **La Grenouillère** (1869).

À BOUGIVAL.

Sketch representing summer at Bougival.

La Grenouillère on Croissy Island (drawing).

Rowing (photo).

Claude Monet: **Boating on the River Epte** (1890).

Gustave Caillebotte: **Rower in Top Hat** (1879).

Fishing party (photo).

Pierre-Auguste Renoir: **Edmond Renoir Fishing**

Rowing at Chatou (photo).

After the Franco-Prussian War and during the Belle Époque, *the Seine and its tributaries became the setting for lively Sunday outings that attracted artists who were enchanted with the endless supply of subjects. Having the advantage of being close to both Paris and the countryside, the riverside villages provided the Impressionists with an abundant source of material for their experiments in painting water and its reflections.*

Young men rowed boats, swam and sailed each other from one river bank to the next. Flexing their rounded biceps and twirling their mustaches they vied with one another to attract new partners to end the day with them at the Bal des Canotiers.

It was at Argenteuil that Manet was "completely overcome by open air painting" while watching Monet at work. Less interested in landscape than his friend, Manet preferred to paint people, against a natural background.

Edouard Manet: **Argenteuil** (1874).

The Bal des Canotiers at Bougival (photo).

Argenteuil gave its brilliantly descriptive name to the most radiant period of Impressionism. Manet, Monet, Renoir and Caillebotte were all fascinated by the colorful sailboat regattas that took place there. As Germain Bazin noted, it was at Argenteuil that these artists discovered with Monet that shadows are not deprivations but mutations of color. Manet painted Monet on his boat-studio—the perfect way for Monet to be at the heart of the shimmering light and its reflections on the water. Manet was particularly successful in creating a Japanese-style foreground in his painting of his brother-in-law: **Boating** (c. 1874). The effect of the whiteness of the man's clothing against the vivid blue of the Seine was praised by art critic and novelist J.K. Huysmans.

In 1887, on the Island of the Grande Jatte, Georges Seurat evoked the undying yet unstable atmosphere of a moment in spring with his pristine and finely glistening vision of the passing of a sailboat and canoe. "The purity of the spectral element is the keystone of this technique," wrote the leader of Neo-Impressionism, among whose followers would be Lucien Pissarro.

Pierre-Auguste Renoir: **The Seine at Argenteuil** (1873).

The river Seine (photo).

Edmond Morin: **The Matelotes et Friture Restaurant, July 1877.**

Edouard Manet: **Boating at Argenteuil** (1871).

Georges Seurat: **The Seine From the Island of the Grande Jatte, Spring** (1887).

Sailboats on the Marne (photo).

Gustave Caillebotte:
Sailboats at Argenteuil (1888).

John Singer Sargent:
Claude Monet Painting
(1887).

Pierre-Auguste Renoir:
**Portrait of
Berthe Morisot.**

Strolling in the meadow (photo).

Berthe Morisot: **Butterfly Chase** (1874).

Claude Monet:
Field of Poppies
(1873).

Camille Pissarro: **The Lock** (1872).

The lock at Bougival (photo).

Alfred Sisley: **Boat at Bougival Lock** (1873).

"The singularity of Berthe Morisot was that she lived her painting and painted her life as if it were a natural and necessary function," Paul Valéry wrote of Manet's sister-in-law. But, in the final analysis, this was the case with all the great Impressionists, for whom the habit of painting became second nature. For many of these artists, their work was the mainstay of their existence.

John Singer Sargent provides a good example of this in his portrait of his friend Monet at the wood's edge: Monet is blended, almost rooted into the forest. And so while Berthe Morisot portrays her sister chasing butterflies, Claude Monet thrusts his wife and son among the poppies, while Pissarro and Sisley stir up breezes and currents as barges pass through the locks. These artists were able to create in the open air without losing a feeling of intimacy. Each artist coordinated his visual experiences with memories of friends' and predecessors' paintings. The painters' exacting metaphysical anguish did not impede the joy of living, which was in the end only a profound need to survive.

In his journal of January 2, 1853, Delacroix noted that "Color is nothing if it doesn't agree with the subject and it doesn't augment the effect of the canvas upon the imagination." One might also add, "and upon the memory."

The Fournaise Hotel-Restaurant at Chatou (photo).

The river banks near the Chatou bridge (photo).

Pierre-Auguste Renoir: **The Chatou Bridge** (1881).

"The train station of Chatou was twenty minutes from Paris and the Fournaise Hotel was just a few minutes from there. Bibesco brought my father there before the (Franco-Prussian) war. Lovers had discovered the area and liked to lose themselves under the large poplar trees. A hotelier from Bougival, Alphonse Fournaise, enlarged one of his buildings and added a landing... Soon Fournaise restaurant became a sort of nautical club... My father had a project to paint a large canvas representing the boaters lunching on the restaurant's terrace. The idea took several years to mature... In 1881 he decided to do it...," related Jean Renoir in **Renoir, My Father.** Auguste Renoir posed, among other friends, the exquisite Alice Charigot (his future wife) playing with a dog opposite the painter and collector Caillebotte who is straddling a chair. Under the canopy we catch a glimpse of the Seine and the bridge that also appears in the background of Renoir's portrait of Alphonsine Fournaise. A miracle of the joy of companionship, this canvas invites us to share with the carefree group their fruit, wine and intimacy.

Pierre-Auguste Renoir:
Alphonse Fournaise (1879).

Pierre-Auguste Renoir:
Alphonsine Fournaise (1879).

Pierre-Auguste Renoir: **The Boatmen's Lunch** (1881).

Boys swimming at La Grenouillère (photo).

Frédéric Bazille: **Summer Scene, Bathers** (1869).

Pierre Puvis de Chavannes: **Hope** (second version).

Robert Demachy: **Nude** (photo).

Heraclitus said that "souls exhale watery substances." Undressed and free, children and adolescents surrender themselves to the water, which is both exalting and soothing. It is as if they are returning to the amniotic fluids of fetal life. Artists such as Puvis de Chavannes rejoiced in seeing the simple and innocent pleasure of those young Venuses emerging from the sea; his own **Hope** was to haunt the pictorial photography of Robert Demachy.

Frédéric Bazille's **Summer Scene, Bathers,** with its beautiful young men, manages to convey a youthful narcissism, stimulated by the summer heat. This naturalistic, spontaneous scene is characteristic of Bazille whose chief aim was the study of figures painted out-of-doors and the relation between the tones of the flesh with those of the landscape.

Seurat, who dreamed of a "democratised Arcadia," found what he was looking for at Asnières, a popular, unsophisticated place for Sunday boating and swimming on the Seine. Seurat composed his **Bathers at Asnières,** a chef-d'œuvre of tranquility and silence, after many painstaking studies evolving towards Pointilism. The sense of expectation and evocation of scorching heat reminds us of Millet. We are plunged into the mood of relaxation and summer vacation.

Artist painting on the river banks (photo).

Georges Seurat: **Une Baignade** (1883-1884).

Gustave Caillebotte: **Diver** (1877).

Mary Cassatt and Gustave Caillebotte, former students of Degas, collected the works of their Impressionist colleagues. Cassatt, a native of Pennsylvania, was responsible for introducing Impressionism to the United States, while Caillebotte donated his collection to France. Artistically, they shared with the Impressionists a determined exactness of draughtsmanship, attenuated by the naive simplicity of the intimist subjects.

Caillebotte, a boating enthusiast, also took hedonistic pleasure in the expression of blossoming nudes whose titles often contained 'Garden' or 'Bathers'. "The nude is an indispensable form of art," confided Renoir to Berthe Morisot. Looking at Renoir's **Bathers,** Morisot ecstatically exclaimed "they charm me as much as Ingres' nudes." Renoir became 'Ingresque' yet at the same time resorted to the antique character of François Girardon's 17th century low relief. Felix Vallotton also referred to this remarkable archaic art in his painting **The Source.**

Bathing at Chatou (photo).

Antony Morlon: **"Ah! What a Pretty Head."**

Mary Cassatt: **Bathing** (1892).

Félix Vallotton: **Bather, or The Source** (1897).

Pierre-Auguste Renoir: **Bathers** (1887).

François Girardon: **Nymphs Bathing** (1675) Low relief.

Pierre-Auguste Renoir:
Young Bather (1892).

Alfred Sisley:
Flood at Pont–Marly
(1876).

'Still waters run deep.' This proverb could have been the motto for the Impressionists and Divisionists; they did all they could to move water, to provide it with ever changing reflections, to make it overflow and invade their meteorological canvases. High and low water marks; ice and snow breaking apart; tides and floods... so much water flowed from their palettes, but it fell drop by drop, touch upon touch, turning into permanent canvases bearing fleeting dreams.

The village of Vétheuil (photo).

Claude Monet: **Vétheuil in Summer** (1880).

With the brilliant appearance in 1888 of his **A Sunday Afternoon on the Island of La Grande Jatte,** *Seurat broke away from Impressionism by using a Divisionist technique (also called Pointilism). This method consisted of reconstructing the effects and shading of light by the juxtaposition of small dots of pure color. This Neo-Impressionism claimed to be scientific and was later codified by Paul Signac who saw a chance of "insuring all the benefits of luminosity, collaboration and harmony." In a portrait of his wife, Signac put this theory into practice by multiplying the specks of the parasol. Seurat's success with this technique might also be attributed to the dead pan humor with which he treated the stiffness of his models. The totally unexpected appearance of the lady holding a monkey on a leash is an example of Seurat's subtle wit. Although the passion for this technique may not have lasted forever, the charm of the painting has endured to this day.*

Georges Seurat: **Sunday Afternoon on the Island of La Grande Jatte** (1884–1886) *See following page.*

Sunday afternoon outing (photo).

Photographic portrait of Madame Signac.

Paul Signac: **Woman with Parasol** (1893).

Emile Bernard and Vincent Van Gogh (from the back) on the quay at Asnières (photo).

Vincent Van Gogh: **The Restaurant de la Sirène, Asnières** (1887).

The Seine at Asnières.

In the Spring of 1887, Émile Bernard met Vincent Van Gogh at the home of père Tanguy, a Montmartre paint-mixer who befriended some of the most innovative painters and collected many of their works. Cézanne, whose parents lived at Asnières, invited his admirers Bernard and Van Gogh to the Sirène restaurant, where they watched one another at work and argued passionately on the quays of the Seine. Van Gogh's works already showed signs of a pre-Fauvist expressionism, and his restrospective in 1901 would have a decisive influence on Derain and Vlaminck. Van Gogh prepared to leave for Arles in the south of France, where he hoped to find the frenzied colors he sought. He invited Émile Bernard to join him, but Bernard was more interested in having Van Gogh introduce him to Paul Gauguin. And so they went their separate ways, Bernard to Brittany to join Gauguin, and Van Gogh to Arles.

Vincent Van Gogh: **The Bateau-Lavoir at Asnières** (1887).

Émile Bernard: **Asnières Bridge** (1887).

Train crossing the Asnières bridge (photo).

Vincent Van Gogh: **Asnières Bridge** (1887).

121

Charles-François Daubigny: **Washerwomen on the Shores of the River Oise** (c. 1855).

Vincent Van Gogh: **Portrait of Doctor Gachet** (1890)

Léonide Bourges: **Daubigny.
Memories and Sketch.**

Camille Pissarro:
**Portrait
of Cézanne.**

Paul Cézanne: **Cézanne Engraving Doctor Gachet** (1873).

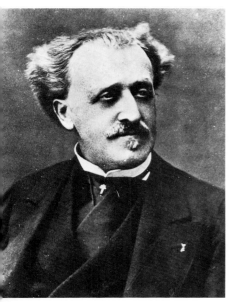

Photographic portrait of Doctor Gachet.

Paul Cézanne: **House of Doctor Gachet, Auvers** (1873-74).

Refusing to paint angelic or pompous paintings, these innovators were often poor but found that a good friend was just as valuable as money. The artists were fortunate enough to have happiness accompanying them on their journey.

One home of such solidarity was found at Auvers-sur-Oise where two sensitive men, Daubigny and Gachet, were the incarnation of this spirit. Daubigny, the creative forerunner of Impressionism, moved to Auvers in 1860 after discovering the mellowness of the river Oise on his boat-studio the 'Botin.' He soon welcomed numerous artists on board, including Pissarro, who lived at nearby Pontoise. In 1872 the eclectic and kind Dr. Gachet moved to Auvers and there opened his heart to many friends. Eighteen years later, at the request of Theo Van Gogh, Dr. Gachet took charge of Vincent, who was suffering from depression. Vincent claimed that his portrait of Dr. Gachet was a "waiting" and a "cry"—a cry less audible than the detonation of the pistol with which he made his escape from his sad, solitary world.

123

Vincent Van Gogh: **Daubigny's Garden** (1890).

Léonide Bourges: **Charles Daubigny.**

Daubigny's garden (photo).

Vincent Van Gogh: **Stairway at Auvers** (1890).

I n his frantic need to grab hold of painting and leave behind the last memories of his internal pain, Vincent executed more than seventy canvases within two months of the summer of 1890. In these works he ran the entire color spectrum, from solar yellow to midnight blue. He hesitated between two choices that branched from Daubigny's garden—the stairway and the church, or the townhall and the wheatfields: a choice between the measured, harsh axis of life, and the gloomy, lofty one of death.

124

The church at Auvers-sur-Oise (photo).

Vincent Van Gogh: **The Church at Auvers-sur-Oise** (1890).

Paul Cézanne: **House of the Hanged Man** (1872-73).

In contrast to Van Gogh, Cézanne, like Susanna fleeing the elders, escaped from this introverted approach and adopted a promising, lucid and clear analysis of the earth and its structure. This search led him to the triumphant summits of Mount Sainte-Victoire.

125

Vincent Van Gogh: **At the Bar,** Auvers-sur-Oise (1890).

The Ravoux Inn at Auvers-sur-Oise (photo, 1890).

Vincent Van Gogh: **Portrait of Adeline Ravoux** (1890).

Jean-François Millet: **Crows in Winter** (1866).

Charles-François Daubigny: **Crows in a Tree** (1867).

Photographic portraits of Arthur-Gustave Ravoux and his daughter Adeline

Vincent Van Gogh: **Crows over a Wheatfield** (1890).

The wheatfield that Van Gogh painted (photo).

On Sunday July 27, 1890, Vincent stole out of the Ravoux Inn after his silent breakfast and went into the fields at Auvers. Here, where he had painted flocks of crows, Vincent shot himself. Neither the untiring love of his brother Theo, nor the prudent solicitude of Dr. Gachet, nor his friendship with the young Adeline Ravoux, could stop him from taking this action. "I've shot myself..." he confirmed to the inn keeper, whose wife and daughter had him alerted after they saw Vincent struggling towards his room. An unfinished letter he was carrying contained his confession: "I have risked my life for my work and my reason is half in the shadows." The other half would be darkened forever on that day. On the 29th of July, around one o'clock in the morning, Vincent died in his brother's arms.

Vincent Van Gogh: **The Garden of Doctor Gachet.**

Joseph Mallord William Turner: **Facade of Rouen Cathedral** (1832).

The portal of Rouen Cathedral (photo).

W hat force and courage, what patience and rage were required to accomplish this feat! From February 1892 until April of the following year, Monet rented a room at the Hotel d'Angleterre and plunged into his paintings of Rouen Cathedral. Inspired by a Turner watercolor he set himself the challenge of faithfully reproducing and reducing the finest modulations of light at different hours of the day, upon the most difficult of elements; the exterior stone of a sacred building which, despite affronts by weather and assaults by man, was the height of nobility. "What difficulties I have in rendering what I feel. I tell myself that whoever thinks that he has finished a canvas is terribly arrogant," he complained. Publicly acclaimed by the art critic Clemenceau, these works also affected Pissarro who, "thrilled by that extraordinary mastery," hastened to put it to the test in his own painting of the **Old Market Place at Rouen.**

Lucien Pissarro: **Camille Pissarro.**

Camille Pissarro: **The Boïeldieu Bridge at Rouen** (1896).

Claude Monet: **Rouen Cathedral, Morning. White Harmony** (1894).

Claude Monet: **Rouen Cathedral, Sunny Morning. Blue Harmony** (1894).

Rouen Cathedral (photo).

Camille Pissarro:
**The Old Market
at Rouen**
(1898).

129

Article in **l'Illustration** on the Salon d'Automne, November 4, 1905.

Henri-Julien Rousseau: **The Hungry Lion Leaps Upon the Antelope...** (1905). Detail.

Stuffed lion and antelope made for the inauguration of the Zoology Gallery at the Museum of Natural History in Paris in 1889.

As indicated by an article in the November 4, 1905 edition of Illustration, *Douanier Rousseau exhibited at the Salon d'Automne that year,* **The hungry Lion,** *inspired by a stuffed lion at the Museum of Natural History in Paris. Surprised by the howling colors and brutal treatment—a revolt against the delicay of Impressionism—the art critic Vauxcelles was not only reacting to this animal scene but also to the paintings of Vlaminck, Derain, Manguin, Matisse, Rouault, and Van Dongen, when he called the exhibition the* Cage aux Fauves *("Wild Animal cage"). The name was a great success and this violent, impetuous, exuberant new form of painting became known as "Fauvism" ("wild beasts"). It was born in different places at the same time, but it took root especially at Chatou, where, in order to work together, Vlaminck and Derain had rented a large room at the Levanneur Restaurant.*

Maurice de Vlaminck: **The Chatou Bridge** (1906).

The 'Wash-boat' at Chatou (photo).

André Derain: **The Seine at Chatou** (1904).

The church at Chatou (photo).

131

Charles Camoin: **Portrait of Marquet** (1904).

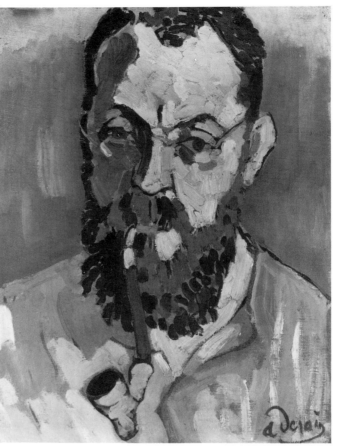

André Derain: **Portrait of Matisse** (1905).

André Derain: **Portrait of Vlaminck** (1905).

Henri Matisse: **Portrait of Derain** (1905).

Said Derain, *"Fauvism is my way of revolting and freeing myself."* In reaction to the hyper-Impressionism, the Fauves had discovered that *"the more basic the means, the more room there is for sensitivity to to appear"* as Gustave Moreau suggested at the École des Beaux-Arts. *Aware of the dynamism that came with mechanization, electricity and the speed of their era, these painters were excited by the brutal fever of harsh color.*

That blaze of excitement reached its height in

1905, but soon diminished and each artist went off in his own direction. Matisse sought to further simplify and refine painting, preferring the graceful rhythm of arabesques and a play of lines to the use of harsh color. Responding to the energy which emanates from the movement of contours, Matisse outlined the figures of women on a beach in **Le Luxe,** *at the same time that Picasso made color submit to form in his studies for the* **Demoiselles d'Avignon.**

Henri Matisse: **Luxe** (1907).

Claude Monet: **Bridge over Lily Pond** (1899).

Bridge over the lily pond at Giverny (1902).

Around 1890 Monet began to work on his garden at Giverny, his final home. He formed a pond by diverting the river Epte and changing its course so that it flowed into his garden. He added a Japanese style footbridge, planted exotic flowers, weeping willows, bamboo trees and rhododendron. His garden became not only a source of personal pleasure ("My finest masterpiece is my garden"), but also the subject of more than seventy canvases. In the beginning they were brilliant exercises in color abstraction, in which he softened the outlines of plants and weeds with a surrounding mist. Later he concentrated on the reflections of the water lilies, trees and foliage in the pond. This series of paintings, begun when Monet was in his seventies, marked the summit of his artistic career. Cézanne, who was staying at an inn in Giverny in the Fall of 1894, said of him, "Monet is only an eye. But what an eye!"

Claude Monet: **Flowered Arch** (1912).

Claude Monet under the arbor at Giverny (photo).

134

Claude Monet: **Waterlilies, Water landscape** (1905).

Claude Monet's shadow on the lily pond (photo).

Claude Monet in his garden at Giverny (photo).

135

4
THE BATIGNOLLES MONTMARTRE
Descending to the Street

Henri de Toulouse-Lautrec: **Artist Painting.**

Gentlemen in detachable collars and haughty top hats cast a severe eye over Valentin le Désossé and his partner as they furiously perform in the *Dance at the Moulin Rouge,* painted by Henri de Toulouse-Lautrec in 1890. Literally turning his back on the conventions of the bourgeoisie, Toulouse-Lautrec sealed the reconciliation of art with the life of the streets: the cabarets, the café-concerts, the people.

Other artists had preceded Toulouse-Lautrec in this fascination with the most earthy and delinquent aspects of Parisian social life. These artists included Gavarni and Guys, who were the subject of Baudelaire's famous articles, "Paintings of Modern Life" and "The Beauty of Circumstances or the Treatment of Morals," published in *Le Figaro* in 1863. But most important was Honoré Daumier, first-rate sleuth of anonymous scenes of the human comedy. This movement was best expressed and most popular during the latter part of the 19th century and the beginning of the 20th, at the crossroads of Batignolles and Montmartre. The artists representing this bohemian world comprised the greatest and the boldest: Manet, Degas, Renoir, Van Gogh, Toulouse-Lautrec, Bonnard, Steinlen, Forain, Picasso and Utrillo…

Henri de Toulouse-Lautrec: **Dance at the Moulin Rouge.** Detail (1890).

137

Browsing in this imaginary museum that makes up such a varied and moving chapter in art history, one cannot help recalling the words of Count Salvandy to the future King Louis-Philippe during festivities at the Royal Palace two months before the 1848 Revolution: "We are dancing on a volcano." Painting at Montmartre boiled in the depths as if in the hollow of a crater; its creators extracted from this neighborhood the most scathing and revolutionary variations. Everyday life and its atmosphere were reinstated as appropriate subjects, having been forgotten in the obsession with nature. The designing of theatrical posters and handbills not only turned publicity itself into art, but actually brought art into the streets.

Astonishing as it may seem (since art historians haven't called much attention to the fact) modern art was really and truly forged at Montmartre. It took shape from the passionate dialogues at the *Martyrs* brasserie or the *Café Guerbois,* the animated debates at the *Café de la Nouvelle-Athènes,* the conversations at the *Lapin Agile* cabaret and the studios at the *Bateau-Lavoir.* (This notion will be explored in greater depth in the last chapter.) These cafés and brasseries were not only a place for the artists to meet but in themselves became the subject of the artists' investigations. The most innovative artists found inspiration in the streets, cafés, launderies, circuses and brothels.

If one had to give a common denominator to all these brilliant or savage, silent or sardonic masters of Montmartre, then spontaneity fits the bill. "An artist must be spontaneous. This is the correct word," affirmed Manet, who preferred this term to 'Impressionist', which was a misnomer for him in any case. It was virtually against his will that his young admirers—Monet, Renoir, Bazille and Astruc—along with Zola, formed a group in his *Batignolles Studio* making him their spokesman during meetings at the nearby *Café Guerbois.*

As frank as Manet, as sensitive to the first—and best—instinct, the Montmartre artists learned about life from the streets and the inhabitants of the Butte. It was a poor and communal school. As Montaigne had said some years before "I would prefer that my son learned to speak at the tavern, rather than learn fine talk at school." One is less likely to cheat people who are one's models. And one fools them less willingly when one has friends like the photographer Nadar, or the writer Zola, and poets like Baudelaire, Mallarmé, Verlaine, Rimbaud or Apollinaire.

It was no longer possible to mystify or romanticize one's subjects, whether they were laborers, loose women, greengrocers, drunkards, street urchins, can-can dancers or bear trainers. Living in a district where one's escorts are alley cats and gutter drunks, one becomes more realistic, and painting becomes more convincing, and—if the case arises—more merciless.

Is it hypocritical to continue painting even when, returning to the studio one day, the artist finds his poor young servant hanging by a rope and reproaches himself, too late, for having unjustly reprimanded the child? There follows the announcement to the boy's pitiable parents, consoling them in a monotone; "After all, it is perhaps for the best; he would have ended badly." And then the mother asks, if it's no problem, could she please have the rope back, in order not to let anything go to waste.

That was Alexandre, irreproachable and blissful as *The Boy with A Dog* and the *Child with Cherries* by Manet.

No one could fool Suzanne Valadon, former trapeze artist, injured in a fall, who was both an artist's model and a painter. She gained insight by posing for painters like Puvis de Chavannes, Renoir, Zandomeneghi, Henner, Utter and Toulouse-

Lautrec and learned that "in order to reach the soul of the model, one must have the courage to look into her face."

The Liberating Spirit of Montmartre

In Montmartre, people knew how to reduce life to its simplest expression, free of all complications: this was how they won the hearts of the artists. This philosophy of life taught the painters, poets and writers who faithfully went there how to become seekers of truth and how to link "the sarcasm of gaiety with the indulgence of contempt." They learned how to turn unhappiness into derision, vice into obsolescence and resignation into habit without ever giving in to remorse. But most of all these artists learned how to persevere.

This was the spirit that captivated Toulouse-Lautrec, who adopted Montmartre in a flash. He would never have considered treating the residents in the manner of the Salon painters, giving them the figures of Greek gods or the charms of Venus. There was no place in the stark reality of Montmartre for this kind of idealization; such an approach would have seemed inappropriate, even shocking, to the locals. And so Lautrec represented this world without sentiment or idealization. His words were as incisive as his paint brushes: "He looks like a fish, both his eyes are on the same side of his nose" (his description of Picasso).

Manet too kept a cool head and despite his reputation of distinguished severity allowed himself to be distracted now and again. A story has it that when his wife discovered him arranging the beautiful legs of a not so innocent model, his immediate response was "It's funny, I thought she was you." His advice to a young painter was "You must remain master and do whatever amuses you."

Manet was eclectic and empirical throughout his life, unlike Degas, who was obsessed with the glory of art and the little ballerinas, prima donnas and prostitutes, or Renoir, who had eyes and paintbrushes only for young girls in their Sunday best, or Lautrec, who felt tall only in the company of long legged dancers or behind the doors of brothels. From one of his first paintings venerating the *Street Singer* and to his last masterpiece dedicated to the memory of the *Bar at the Folies-Bergère,* Manet made no distinction between tarts and flirts, comediennes and tragediennes, as long as they had some quality that could be translated into painting. He never hesitated to approach a potential model. A friend relates how "At the entrance of Guyot Street, there was a woman leaving a cabaret, adjusting her clothes and carrying a guitar. He went right up to her and asked her to come and pose for him at his studio." Manet's eyes were pledged to the flow of humanity—in the streets or in solitude.

Meeting, Conversation, Mediation

Honoré de Balzac observed "Oh Paris! Anyone who does not admire your dark landscapes, your gleaming light, your deep and silent *cul-de-sacs;* who does not hear your murmurs between midnight and dawn, knows nothing of real poetry…"

Perhaps this is what the citizens of Montmartre attempted to tell their intrigued visitors—simply that the street is life, the road to the Other. In Montmartre, the cheap open-air cafés replaced the salons, the arbors and bistros the Opéra, the railroad station bars the frontiers to the New World, the Commune barricades the royal mausoleum and the song "Cherry Season" the only requiem. Everything was bliss, or at least an excuse for an early drink to combat desire, to forget lost causes or to see life through rose-tinted glasses. Through intoxication the artists discovered life's Bacchanalian fantasies which made the future remote. Like Baudelaire, it helped them to dream of the Great Evening:

"One evening, the wine's soul sang in the bottle:

Mankind, I'm straining towards you

Oh dear disinherited.

Under my prison of glass

and ruby wax

A song full of light and fraternity."

This was the song of the painters of Batignolles and the Butte of Montmartre. They were amused, moved and conquered by these lines, noted and stored away in their memories. Why did these bitter, precise and nostalgic individuals take refuge in those places? Where did they come from? How did Montmartre come to be that city of the arts?

In order to understand the origins of that nocturnal and versatile studio that was Montmartre, it is necessary to go back to King Louis-Philippe. How was the King responsible for that progressive migration toward Paris's oldest, most neglected pleasure ground and the artists' reconquest of the streets? His influence was twofold. His granting of political and economic power to the bourgeoisie gave them inordinate authority which they wielded until the institution of the Third Republic. They used this power to control art through the official Salons and to impose their conventional tastes on the people. At the same time, not wishing to appear as a "shadowy accomplice," the king, on December 31, 1836, closed those dens of iniquity within the Royal Palace galleries that had attracted the most famous gamblers in the world and had inevitably led to the opening of the most beautiful cafés in Paris. As a result, the cafés took to the large avenues northwest of Paris. Soon the word spread and painters went to Batignolles and climbed the hills of Montmartre to find open-air cafés.

Naturally, prostitutes accompanied this exodus, and then, gradually, the impoverished apprentices, and grisettes followed, under the surveillance of ruffians. They began sauntering near the railway stations and around the Notre-Dame-de-Lorette. Nicknamed 'lorettes', these women were more appealing to artists than those solemn spouses of the upper middle class, installed in their chic salons.

The Café Banner

Beer, imported from Germany, became a fashionable drink around 1853 and brasseries soon sprang up. Waiters were replaced by bar maids who often moonlighted as prostitutes, causing substantial harm to the brothels, whose number declined from 194 in 1860 to 59 in 1892. The 'singing cafés', born at the beginning of the Second Empire, also took the same route to Montmartre. "You are happy. You sing, drink, smoke and keep your hat on so as not to catch cold." Soon café concerts, cabarets, dance halls and circuses multiplied throughout Montmartre.

Artists of every political and social background found cheap lodgings, studios, models and diversions among good friends at Batignolles and Montmartre. They invaded the taverns and climbed the winding paths leading to the Place du Tertre.

Balzac once said that "Cafés have banners and one judges a Parisian's opinion by the café he frequents." This was as true of the artists and writers as it was of Balzac's politicians. If one considers the *Café Guerbois,* on the main street of Batignolles or the *Café Nouvelle Athènes* at Pigalle as cradles of Impressionism, then, to be fair, one must also pay homage to the sources of art that remained anonymous. These would include the bars and taverns, humble as the people who haunted them, from which these compassionate and comradely artists extracted paintings with all the colors of life acting as banners. Banners which will always be international.

Edouard Manet: **Portrait of Emile Zola** (1868).

"**D**on't do what I do. Don't do what others have done." This precept was aimed at the formalist teachings of the École des Beaux Arts *(School of Fine Arts) and would progressively give rise to the liberal conception of collective studios. Independent masters such as Couture, Suisse, Julian and Gleyre (whose studio was a meeting place for Renoir, Monet, Bazille and Sisley), were witnesses to the beginnings of unprecedented careers. Can one create without sharing? Even in their solitude, painters as unique as Lautrec needed to get their bearings at Cormon's studio.*

The most important of these personal studios was Manet's at Batignolles, which Fantin-Latour painted, depicting the artist and his friends in the company of Zola. Manet paid tribute to Zola's courageous defense of early Impressionism by painting the novelist at his desk, surrounded by Japanese prints and the artist's own scandalous **Olympia.**

In lending his studio to the Impressionists for their first exhibition in 1874, the photographer Nadar proved that he was as clairvoyant as Zola.

Emile Zola (photo).

Edouard Manet (photo).

Henri Fantin-Latour: **Studio at Batignolles** (1870).

Nadar's studio at 35 Blvd des Capucines (photo).

Cormon's studio in 1885. Toulouse-Lautrec is standing at the far left (photo).

Toulouse-Lautrec
by himself.

Toulouse-Lautrec painting **The Dance at the Moulin Rouge** in his studio (1890).

Frédéric Bazille: **Painter's Studio** (1870).

Edouard Vuillard: **Portrait of Thadée Natanson.**

Pierre-Auguste Renoir: **Painter's Studio** (1876).

Armand Guillaumin: **Martinez in Guillaumin's Studio** (1878).

The popularity of the literary cafés of Batignolles, the liveliness of Montmartre and its street activity, had a fresh appeal for the promising artists who ventured there. Rebelling against the rigidity of the École des Beaux Arts, as typified by the classes led by Bonnat, these artists preferred the bohemian atmosphere of the streets. There they found the subjects for their canvases among the street urchins, casual young women and feline dandies. They also learned about life's deceptions, desires, cruelties and candor while mingling with the people of these quarters.

Bonnat's studio at the **École des Beaux-Arts** in 1890.

The rue Cortot and rue Mont-Cenis in Montmartre. Mimi Pinson's house (photo).

Maximilien Luce: **Suzanne Valadon's House** (1895).

Rosimond's house in Montmartre.

Suzanne Valadon: **Rue Cortot.**

And so the artists moved to Montmartre. Bazille settled near the Café Guerbois and Renoir lived first at rue Saint-Georges, then climbed to the rue Cortot where Suzanne Valadon lived with her son Utrillo.

This move to Montmartre did not rule out the need to escape to the countryside from time to time. And when, around 1900, the artists began descending toward Montparnasse, they enthusiastically accepted invitations, such as that of Thadée Nathanson, to visit the surrounding villages.

145

Gustave Caillebotte: **The Café** (1880).

Edouard Manet: **The Beer-waitress** (1879).

Edouard Manet: **Interior of Café Guerbois** (1869).

Jean-Louis Forain: **Café.**

Café terrace (photo).

The heroes in Zola's The Dram-Shop *took comfort in cabarets and cafés. In these cabarets flowing with ale and absinthe, everyone drank, as Verlaine put it, "without thirst to future friendship." These cafés transformed jests into slogans, the most fearful toasts into loving tributes and the most innocent women into tigresses. Many friendships and secret liaisons were made in these places where the painters searched for their identities. They could choose from among the Martyrs brasserie the Tortoni Café, the Café de Bade, the brasserie Richschoffen, the Grande Pinte, the Café Riche or the Café Guerbois. The ambiance and the people of the cafés and brasseries became the subjects of novels and poems as well as paintings by Caillebotte, Manet and Degas. These were perfect settings in which to try out new techniques and experiment with lighting and contrast.*

Edouard Manet: **At Père Lathuille's** (1879).

Frédéric Regamey:
Gervaise and Coupeau.
Illustration for
The Dram-Shop (1878).

Photographic portrait
of Guy de Maupassant.

Edgar Degas: **Women on a Café Terrace** (1877).

147

Edouard Manet: **The Plum** (1877).

Photographic portrait of Ellen Andrée.

Paul Verlaine with a glass of absinthe (photo).

This group of artists, sometimes referred to as the 'Batignolles Group' tackled their naturalistic and pluralistic views on art at the Café Guerbois *under the leadership of Manet. However, after 1870 they switched to the Nouvelle-Athènes where they were soon joined by a great many other artists. Verlaine's description of this period as a time when "life became easy and took on a sharp and coarse flavor… without gaiety or remorse," is borne out in paintings by Manet and Degas, and Lautrec and Zandomeneghi. Ellen Andrée posed for both* **The Plum** *and* **Absinthe,** *just as Suzanne Valadon was the model for both the* **Woman Drinking** *and* **At the Café de la Nouvelle Athènes.** *Each artist had his own particular insight into this libertine world.*

Edgar Degas: **Absinthe Drinkers** (1876).

Henri de Toulouse-Lautrec:
The Hangover (1889).

The Nouvelle Athènes Café (photo).

Edgar Degas: **The Nouvelle Athènes Café** (1878).

Federico Zandomeneghi: **At the Nouvelle Athènes Café** (1885).

Photograph of Yvette Guilbert, the Queen of the **Divan Japonais.**

Henri de Toulouse-Lautrec: **Poster for the Divan Japonais** (1892

Henri de Toulouse-Lautrec: **Yvette Guilbert Taking A Curtain Call.**

Edgar Degas:
Singer in Black Gloves (1878).

Ferdinand Lunel: **Interior of the Divan Japonais.**

Henri Somm: **Illustrated menu for the Rat Mort Cabaret** (1884).

Lautrec was as fascinated by the artificial and nocturnal life of the entertainment world, as his Impressionist friends were by their sun-cloaked world. Like Degas, but in a more caricatured, flaunting style, Lautrec focuses our attention on the gestures, the tics, the naive as well as affected expressions of the singers and dancers in the artificial gas light. "But for Heaven's sake don't make me so atrociously ugly! Not everyone sees the exclusively artistic side," begged Yvette Guilbert, a singer at the Divan Japonais cabaret.

"One never knew whether it was the music that made the beer flow or the beer that helped you swallow the music," was Daumier's comment on the spectacles at the café-concerts. Will we ever understand the fascination the performers held for these night owls, these expressionist and bizarre painters? What was there about the dancer from the Rat Mort (Dead Rat) cabaret that so electified Vlaminck?

Maurice de Vlaminck: **Dancer from the Rat Mort** (1906).

Honoré Daumier:
Café-Concert.

Pierre–Auguste Renoir: **Country Dance** (1883).

Théophile Steinlen: **The 14th of July Dance.**

Degas, Renoir and Steinlen, whose hearts belonged to Montmartre, find each other in the festivities on this double page. Full of good humor, they were united by their parallel realism. Instinctively sympathetic with the cocky working class, described by de Maupassant as the "core of our race," the artists were moved by the apprentice dressmakers and delivery boys who let themselves go in the swing of an accordian waltz. And when one of the street singers poured out her heart about "those poor guys in love with someone who don't love them" tears flowed down the faces of the most cynical members of the audience. Degas described Théresa, one of the most popular of these street singers: "She opens her rather large mouth and out comes one of the roughest yet most spiritually tender voices in existence." It was at Bougival that Renoir waltzed his friend Paul Lhote with Alice Charigot in the **Country Dance,** and his brother with Suzanne Valadon in the **Dance at Bougival.**

A 14th of July dance at Montmartre (photo).

Edgar Degas: **Café-Concert Singer** (1875-77).

In the spring of 1876, Renoir began making trips from his studio to the nearby Moulin de la Galette, the setting for his large canvas **Dancing at the Moulin de la Galette.** *He engaged his friends to help him carry the canvas and to pose for him. It was a perpetual game of hide-and-seek with the sun, in which Renoir was the victor.*

In love with love itself and all varieties of friendship and affection, these artists were as free as air; they lived by no other law than the taking of pleasure. Renoir dissolved them in fluttering, tantalizing light.

When **Dancing at the Moulin de la Galette** *appeared at the Third Impressionist Exhibition, most of the art critics savagely attacked it for its "cadaver-like effects." Fortunately the faithful Caillebotte came to the rescue and bought it, thereby confirming that he believed in the immortality of this painting dedicated to youth, light and joy.*

Pierre-Auguste Renoir: **Le Moulin de la Galette** (1876).   Frédéric Bazille: **Portrait of Renoir** (1867).

Vincent Van Gogh: **Le Moulin de la Galette seen from rue Girardon** (1886).

Montmartre artist painting the Moulin de la Galette (photo).

The field below the Moulin (photo).

What painter, living or passing through Montmartre, was not tempted, like some Don Quixote, to attack the large crossed arms of the windmills of the Butte?

The first windmills of Montmartre date back to the 13th century. Their owners, who used them more as living quarters than as mills, began serving drinks. From 1640 on, people began dancing there.

The most celebrated and resilient of Montmartres' windmills was the Moulin de la Galette. This landmark was valiantly defended against the Cossacks by its proprietors, the Debrays, and was much depicted by artists. Corot, Rousseau, Renoir, Lautrec, Van Gogh, Picasso, Steinlen, Utrillo and Van Dongen are just a few of the painters who portrayed this mill throughout its many ages. Originally called the "Blute-in" (The Fine Sieve) its name changed in 1834 when père Debray began to sell galettes (round flat cakes made of puff pastry). He added an open-air café and a dancing area, where he taught his famous "entrechat."

Théophile Steinlen: **Montmartre Windmills** (1903).

Maurice Utrillo: **Le Moulin de la Galette** (1913).

The Moulin de la Galette (photo).

Marcel Leprin:
Le Moulin de la Galette (1918).

157

Roedel: **Poster for the Moulin de la Galette.**

Entrance to the Moulin de la Galette.

Federico Zandomeneghi: **Le Moulin de la Galette** (1878).

The Moulin de la Galette became very popular in the 1870s. With its new canopy and large dance hall, it lost some of the good-natured ambiance that Renoir had so joyfully depicted and took on a sleazier atmosphere, which immediately attracted Lautrec. The swinging rhythms of quadrilles, waltzes and polkas soon evoked the mood of a mob on a binge. Shop assistants, laundresses, apprentices, factory workers, prostitutes and their pimps and of course artists like Lautrec, Van Dongen, and later Picasso, drank, danced, flirted and made conquests amidst the blaring music.

Pablo Picasso: **Le Moulin de La Galette** (1900).

Henri de Toulouse-Lautrec: **Dance at the Moulin de la Galette** (1889).

The new dance hall at the Moulin de la Galette (photo 1898).

Kees Van Dongen:
Le Moulin de la Galette (1904).

159

Henri de Toulouse-Lautrec: **Poster of Jane Avril** (1893).

Photograph of Jane Avril dancing.

The Place Blanche and entrance to the Moulin Rouge (photo).

Georges Redon: **The Place Blanche on the Night of a Ball.**

From the day of its opening in October 1889, the Moulin Rouge monopolized Parisian night life from the Place Blanche.

Lines of hackney coaches discharged wealthy foreigners, diamond-covered duchesses and top-hatted princes. Parisian society was soon followed by artists eager to exploit this new source of painting. Chéret designed the first poster; Willette decorated the walls; Steinlen and the newly-arrived Picasso made lively sketches. Fauves such as Chabaud and Camoin, and Nabis (a Hebrew word meaning "Prophets") such as Bonnard, captured its ghostly scarlet lighting. But Toulouse-Lautrec was more at home here than any of the others. Seated at his table among insolent singers and exhausted dancers, Lautrec celebrated the Moulin Rouge in numerous posters, pastels, lithographs and paintings. The Japanese staging, merry colors and bold outlines of these works emphasized the social and psychological truthfulness of a world gone mad in the throes of delirious pleasure.

Pablo Picasso:
Self Portrait in front of the Moulin Rouge (1901).

Auguste Chabaud: **Le Moulin Rouge at Night** (1905).

161

Henri de Toulouse-Lautrec: **Mlle. Eglatine's Dancers** (1896).

La Goulue and Grille d'Égout (photo).

Dance at the Moulin Rouge (photo).

Can-can dancers at the Moulin Rouge (photo).

Henri de Toulouse-Lautrec: **La Goulue Entering the Moulin Rouge** (1891-92).

The viscount Henri de Toulouse-Lautrec took enormous pleasure in sharing his noble quarters with the singer Jane Avril and her chorus of can-can dancers. What a collection: Grille d'Égout ("sewer grill") so called because of her gapped teeth; Nini-Feet-in-the-Air; Death-Dodger and Cricri, who almost killed herself executing an enthusiastic cartwheel; the Crayfish Kid whose specialty was dancing backwards; Flying-in-the Wind who made hats soar with a kick of her boot and the Glutton who drank anything and everything that was left on the tables. There is no doubt that Lautrec adopted these women because they were able to hear the heart of gold that beat in his dwarfed body. This heart beat to the same rhythm as that of Valentin-le-Désossé when he let himself go in the **Dance at the Moulin Rouge**.

162

Henri de Toulouse-Lautrec: **The Dance at the Moulin Rouge** (1890).

A young woman pasting posters in Montmartre.

Ah! the Folies-Bergère! "The only place in Paris which smells deliciously of both the powder of bought caresses and the weariness of corruption," was Huysmans' description.

Ill and, sensing his imminent death, Manet concentrated all his experiences of Spanish, Classical, Realist and Impressionist painting into this work. Suzon, the barmaid from the Folies-Bergère, came to his studio and posed before a large mirror in which Manet reflected his memories of that lively gaslit café. One sees the shimmering reflections in the chandelier, on the bottles of English beer and French champagne. Everything is here, from the little green feet of the trapeze artist in the upper left hand corner to the blemished skin of the painter Latouche. One could take ten pages to comment on this canvas—brilliant swan song—in which Suzon's gaze seems filled with regret at seeing this great artist nearing his end. However, his spirit lived on.

Bonnard, after being admitted to the School of Fine Arts, threw himself into artistic life by dedicating his first poster (1889) to champagne —the source of pictorial intoxication.

Pierre Bonnard: **Poster for France-Champagne** (1889).

Edouard Manet: **Bar at the Folies-Bergère** (1881–82).

Maximilien Luce: **Rue des Abbesses** (1896).

From 1880 to 1900, it was in Montmartre and Batignolles, with their narrow lanes and provincial streets, that art took to the outdoors. Merchants defied the seasons and sold their wares on the sidewalks; the aristocracy took its daily five o'clock stroll; tightlipped society matrons looked down their noses at working girls; cabbies trotted through the streets while elderly gentlemen hobbled after them; newspaper vendors hawked their papers; and errand boys and shop girls stole kisses between chores. "Ah! how beautiful was my village, my Paris, my old Paris!" Each artist found his own satisfaction and astonishment in these streets so full of subjects for their canvases.

Market at the corner of rue des Abbesses and rue Lepic (photo).

Pierre Bonnard: **Woman with Umbrella** (1900).

Félix Vallotton: **The Downpour** (1879).

166

Jean-François Raffaelli: **Boulevard des Italiens.**

Street scene (photo).

General view of Boulevard Montmartre (photo).

Théophile Steinlen: **Carriages.**

Camille Pissarro:
Boulevard Montmartre (1897).

Henri de Toulouse-Lautrec: **At the Salon of the rue des Moulins** (1894).

Edgar Degas: **The Brothel, Waiting.**

Edgar Degas: **The Brothel, The Client.**

I f Degas portrayed the world of prostitutes and their clients as though glimpsed through a keyhole, then one can say that Lautrec was on the other side of the door, installed in total complicity.

The shutters and alcoves of the brothels were opened wide to Lautrec who was as familiar with the rue des Moulins as Degas was with the Opera. "Ah now, Lautrec, one can see that you're quite at home there" remarked the impressed master of the ballet classes.

Lautrec and one of his models
in front of his painting (photo).

Women at the rue des Moulins (photo).

Henri de Toulouse-Lautrec: **Women of the rue des Moulins** (1894).

L autrec was fascinated by the
activity, and the vice, that took
place behind the gas-lit shutters
on streets like the rue des Moulins.

In 1894 he moved into a brothel on
this street and produced a series of
paintings and lithographs of its
inhabitants. For Lautrec these women
were "alive... they are so lacking in
pretension..."

Lautrec's understanding treatment of
these women gives an intimate look at
their life without being sentimental or
moralistic. This dispassionate attitude
was shared some years later by Georges
Rouault.

Georges Rouault:
Young Woman at a Mirror (1906).

169

Honoré Daumier: **Laundress.**

Laundresses during the First Empire (photo).

Henri de Toulouse-Lautrec: **Laundress** (1889).

D aumier was the first to study the laboring class in the light and shadow of its hardworking life. He opened the way for a sympathetic realism tinged with the "character and goodness that saves and makes a Daumier," as Pissarro said. Like Daumier, Degas, Lautrec, Forain, Steinlen and Picasso hesitated between satire, anger and dreams. These artists, each in his own way, explored the lives of Montmartre's poor.

Throughout his life Degas spent much time roaming the streets, watching the laundresses at work, studying the glow of kerosene lamps on the pale faces and shroud-like sheets. The women, young and old, who toiled in the launderies were also subjects for Lautrec, and for Picasso during his Blue Period.

André Gill:
Gervaise Counting the Linen. Illustration from *The Dram-Shop* (1878).

Théophile Steinlen:
Laundresses;
Illustration for
the magazine *Rire*.

The rue Saint-Vincent (photo).

Pablo Picasso: **Woman Ironing** (1904).

Edgar Degas: **Laundresses** (1884).

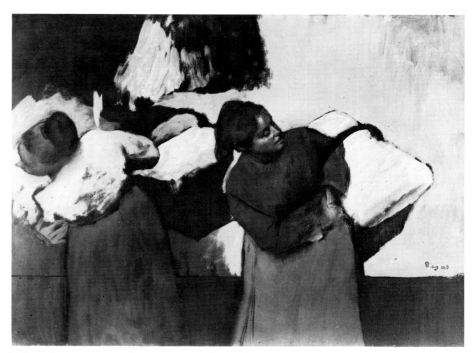

Edgar Degas: **Laundresses Carrying Linen** (1876-78).

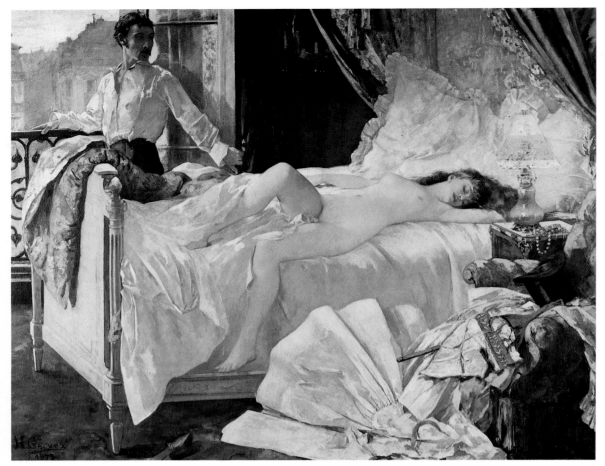

Henri Gervex: **Rolla** (1878).

Braquehars: **Nude Lying on a Divan** (photo of 1854).

Edgar Degas:
Drawing of a semi-nude.

T he mysterious union of poetry and painting can be seen in the sensual visions based upon amorous poems. The story of Don Juan, promising a dream of redemption through love, inspired the poet de Musset, and later the artist Gervex, who made it the subject of his celebrated **Rolla.**

In 1900, the art dealer Ambroise Vollard commissioned Bonnard to illustrate Verlaine's poems Parallelement. Perhaps it was Bonnard's **Indolent,** which evokes the languid mood of Verlaine's poems, that prompted Vollard to choose him as illustrator.

Apollinaire met Picasso at the Bateau Lavoir around the time that he had finished his Chanson du Mal–Aimé. This poem was a favorite of Picasso who dedicated his **Embrace** to his "Dear friend Guillaume Apollinaire."

Pierre Bonnard: **The Lovers.**

Pablo Picasso: **The Embrace** (1905).

Pierre Bonnard: **Indolent** (c. 1899).

Henri de Toulouse-Lautrec: **The Dram-Shop** (1900).

Jean-Louis Forain: **Darn! My table is taken...**

With his great love of painting, Émile Zola dreamed of a brotherhood of genius. In his review of the Salon of 1868 Zola said of his friends: "They form a group which grows everyday. They are at the head of the (modern) movement in art, and tomorrow one will have to reckon with them." Writing to encourage his childhood friend Paul Cézanne, who he knew had a willing heart, he wrote "There are two men in an artist: the poet and the worker... all you have to do to succeed is put your fingers to work."

No matter what their backgrounds or origins, those artists passing through Montmartre communicated that same "pity which makes one even more determined," that Apollinaire praised in the works of Picasso. "He has seen humane images floating in azure memories and participating in divinity."

Théophile Steinlen: **Rue Caulaincourt.**

Water carriers on rue des Saules in Montmartre (photo).

Georges Rouault: **The Couple** (1905).

Pablo Picasso: **Mother and Child** (1903).

Henri de Toulouse-Lautrec: **Laundress** (1889).

The Butte of Montmartre (photo).

Woman near windmill on Montmartre (photo).

Théophile Steinlen: **Poster for the Chat Noir** (1896).

Chinese shadow puppets at the **Chat Noir.**

The **Chat Noir** cabaret (photo).

Adolphe Willette: **Parce Domine** (1884).

Henri de Toulouse-Lautrec: **Aristide Bruant in his Cabaret.**

Photographic portrait of Aristide Bruant.

Aristide Bruant's cabaret (photo).

"I *seek my fortune at the Black Cat in Montmartre by moonlight…" That lively refrain echoed throughout the streets of Montmartre! After obtaining his audience's attention by shouting "Shut your mouths, I'm going sing!," Aristide Bruant broke into his famous "Ballad" at the cabaret. Starting out at the cabaret of the humourist Rudolphe Salis, Bruant took it over in 1885; thus was born the Mirliton cabaret.*

Parce Domine, *the surrealistic minuet painted by Willette for the Black Cat, gives an idea of the wild gaiety that reigned among the journalists, politicians, singers, librettists, poets and painters. A group of the Black Cat's patrons collaborated on a satirical magazine and on comic spectacles of the famous Chinese shadow puppets.*

Among its artist regulars were Seurat and Signac. Lautrec preferred Bruant's Mirliton cabaret and his unforgettable songs, "At Batignolles," "At the Villette" and "Rue Saint-Vincent."

Interior of the Mirliton cabaret. Illustration in 1891 edition of **La Plume.**

177

Edgar Degas: **Miss Lala at the Fernando Circus** (1879).

Henri de Toulouse-Lautrec: **Flying Trapeze.**

"Paris, sad city, turn your eyes toward the circus where one sees the prestige of art united by the accompaniment of your lyre."

The call of Victor Hugo, in one of his Odes, was heard for nearly a century by all the artists who identified with circus life.

Wrestlers and jugglers, tightrope walkers, trapeze artists, horseback riders and clowns lost themselves in the spectacle and saw Fortune smile at their boldness. Here under the tents they conquered their principle obstacle—stage fright. And the great paintings were the risks taken by artists who dared to bare their souls in the same way.

Poster for the Fernando Circus.

Group of acrobats (photo).

Honoré Daumier: **Wrestlers** (1852).

Pierre Bonnard:
The Clown.

Blanche Allarty-Molier horsewoman (photo).

Georges Seurat: **Circus** (1891).

Pablo Picasso: **Galloping Horse** (1905).

Henri de Toulouse-Lautrec:
Fernando Circus (1888).

179

The Medrano Circus (photo).

The painters' favorite circus was the Medrano, located in Montmartre at the corner of the rue des Martyrs and Boulevard Rochechouart. Originally a fairground, the Fernando Circus was rebuilt and subsequently named for one of its clowns —Medrano. Artists were delighted by the crazy antics of the clowns and the rich colors of their setting. And yet, according to Suarès, the clown's art is neither hilarious nor heart—rending: "It is the comic mirror of tragedy and the tragic mirror of comedy." Picasso understood and portrayed this tragicomic aspect in his moving depictions of the circus people. He painted them without artifice, catching them in moments when nonsense is forgotten and what remains is a profoundly human and maternal tenderness.

Photograph of a clown in 1900.

Max Jacob: **At the Circus** (1912).

Kees Van Dongen: **The Clown** (1905).

Pierre-Auguste Renoir: **The Clown** (1868).

Pablo Picasso: **Family of Acrobats with an Ape** (1905).

Vincent Van Gogh: **Woman with Tambourines** (1887).

Henri de Toulouse-Lautrec: **Rice Powder** (1899).

Henri de Toulouse-Lautrec: **A la Mie** (1891).

Maurice Guibert posing for **A la Mie** (photo).

At the end of the century many of the various trends in art converged at Montmartre. Impressionists, Post-Impressionists, Nabis, and Fauves mingled and exchanged ideas that would lead towards one of the most far reaching revolutions in art—Cubism.

One important meeting place was père Tanguy's shop, where artists bought their paints and admired his collection of paintings hanging on the walls. Tanguy's was the only place where one could see Cézanne's work, since the artist had refused to exhibit in Paris since 1887.

Vincent Van Gogh painted the arbor of the **Billards de Paris** restaurant in 1886, at the nearby Place du Tertre. Together with Lautrec, Gauguin, Bernard and Anquetin, Van Gogh organized, at the Tambourine Cabaret, an exhibition that he called "Painters of the Little Boulevard." Agostina Segatori, the owner of the Tambourine, modeled for Van Gogh's **Woman with Tambourines.** She also served as a model for Lautrec, who caught her in a pensive mood. Picasso painted her two years later seated at a table with a siphon and glass.

182

Vincent Van Gogh: **Open-Air Café at Montmartre** (1886).

Pablo Picasso: **The Aperitif** (1901).

I n 1896 Cézanne spent some time in Montmartre. His efforts to reconstruct painting had progressed and the **Harlequins** and **Card Players,** which he had painted in Aix-en-Provence, in the south of France, were products of this new approach. Cézanne wrote that the southern landscapes were like "a playing card, red roofs against the blue sea." and that "to paint is to seize the harmony between the numerous relations."

In the Fall of 1895, after an absence of almost ten years, he sent one hundred and fifty canvases to the young picture dealer, Ambroise Vollard, for an exhibition. Although the public and the critics alike were horrified, young artists such as Maurice Denis and Émile Bernard appreciated these new developments. Six years later, in 1901, Picasso held his own first exhibition at Vollard's gallery.

Paul Cézanne: **Card Players** (1892–1896).

5
PONT-AVEN
LE POULDU
The Spell of Brittany

Paul Gauguin: **Self Portrait with Yellow Christ** (1889).

"**A**FTER FORDING THE RIVER, Jacob went to rest alone, but a stranger came in the night and wrestled with him till dawn. Realizing that he couldn't win, the stranger said to Jacob: "Let me go, daybreak is coming."—"I will not let you go until you have blessed me," replied Jacob. "What is your name?" "Jacob." "Your name will no longer be Jacob, but Israel, because you have wrestled with God and men and you have won…"

Paul Gauguin imagined that the credulous Bretons of Pont-Aven, on hearing this astonishing story would receive his *Vision after the Sermon* as a miracle from the heavens. However, neither the rector of Pont-Aven, nor the one of nearby Nizon, accepted Gauguin's generous offer to donate this painting to their churches.

Gauguin had hoped to consecrate that incredible hand-to-hand combat as Delacroix had done with his murals on the same subject at Saint-Sulpice in Paris. Gauguin wanted to restore the supernatural impulse and symbolic force of expression to art. This desire to reinstate that supremacy to art accompanied Gauguin throughout the several seasons that he spent in Brittany. It was a stuggle that he would share in the happy company of a group of artists.

Paul Gauguin: **The Vision After the Sermon.** Detail (1888).

The *Vision after the Sermon* was Gauguin's declaration of independence. It marked his break with the naturalism of the Impressionists. Although he had painted with Cézanne and Pissarro and exhibited with the Impressionists, he disdained their looking for "what is near the eye, and not at the mysterious heart of thought..."

"My advice—don't copy too much from nature. Art is an abstraction, derive it from nature by dreaming in the presence of nature; think more about creation than the result," was the counsel that Gauguin gave to his young friend Émile Schuffenecker. "I have sacrificed everything this year, including execution and color, to style... It is, I believe, a transformation which hasn't as yet borne any results—but it will." To which he added, "I know that I will be less and less understood."

And yet, in August of 1888, Gauguin, along with Émile Bernard, took the decisive step and repudiated the effete touch of Impressionism and the "little dots" of those he called the "chemist-painters." From now on color was bordered by a new frame, an idea borrowed from cloisonné enamel work in which fine strips of metal are used to outine the enamel areas. Gauguin and Bernard had discovered this technique through the ceramist Chaplet. They also became interested in the effects of the stained glass they saw in the churches in Brittany. In his *Souvenirs* Émile Bernard wrote: "The simplification, or synthesis, imposes itself on the idea as inherent. In painting from memory, I had the advantage of abolishing useless complications of forms and tones. Only an outline of what was seen remains. All lines revert to their geometric architectures; all tones to the prismatic colors of the palette. Then one need only simplify: one must rediscover the origins of everything."

In Search of Eden

The aim of the artists who followed Gauguin was to return to the origins of the world and the source of inspiration. Gauguin led Bernard, Sérusier, Filiger, Verkade, Seguin, Meyer de Haan, Slewinski, Willumsen, O'Conor, Maufra, Moret and Denis to the Bois d'Amour (Wood of Love) at Pont-Aven. The Bois d'Amour where the wind sighed around the islolated farms and in the worn-out wells; where desolate crosses announced gloomy chapels and ravens surveyed the golden dunes.

Why Pont-Aven? What did they find there?

At the end of the 19th century when the mood was pragmatic and myth was replaced by scientific scepticism, many artists and writers looked longingly toward Brittany. Its rugged and wild coastline, and culture steeped in Celtic folklore and legends, offered an exciting alternative to those wishing to escape the influence of the industrial age. These artists explored and excavated the savage coasts, lonely villages and ghostly forests in search of new material for their imagination.

In his *Memories of Childhood and Youth,* published in 1883, Ernest Renan had described himself as having the "soul of a barbarian Celt." And Gustave Flaubert had written a story about his voyage in Brittany where he discovered "the human form in its native freedom, such as it was on the first day of the world." This was the same marvellous Celtic spirit that had been discovered in the 1840's by the Pre-Raphaelite painters in England.

And so, intrigued and excited by the prospect of discovering the wild beauty of the countryside and the ancient culture of its inhabitants, artists and intellectuals left Paris for Brittany in search of this Eden.

Orphan of Impressionism

"**I** arrived as a calm orphan
My only riches were my tranquil eyes."

These lines from Verlaine, which Gauguin copied into his moving *Notebook for Aline,* dedicated to his daughter, summed up his feelings as he arrived at the Gloanec Pension at Pont-Aven in 1888. Gauguin could be described as the orphan of his Impressionist fathers, whom he rejected. In Brittany he broke away from their influence, which had left him feeling frustrated and powerless. Now he and his fellow painters set up their paint boxes on the monolithic stones and allowed the unexpected colors of the sorcerer's landscape to bewitch them.

"I love Brittany. Here I've found the primitive wilderness. When my wooden shoes echo on the granite earth, I hear the dull and mighty muted sounds which I seek in my canvases." These were the sounds that he urged his companions listen to. In the Bois d'Amour, ancient forest of the druids, Gauguin gave his famous lesson in Synthesism to Sérusier. He asked Sérusier to select the most vivid flowers to compose a bouquet of pure color which the future Nabis would call the Talisman. Like Sérusier, the other followers learned Breton songs and dances and transformed them into paintings under the leadership of Gauguin.

Penetrating the Character of the People and Countryside

After a long and tortuous voyage by train, which left them in the medieval city of Quimperlé, the enthusiastic artists covered the remaining 13 miles to Pont-Aven in coaches. At Pont-Aven they were warmly welcomed by Marie Pape, waitress at the Gloanec Pension. Wearing pointed headdresses and broad smiles, the maids ushered the tired and hungry travelers into the dining room where they were revitalized with food and drink. The odor of wax mingled with that of gorse and cider and sardines fried in butter...

Having gone to Pont-Aven in order to "penetrate the character of the people and the countryside," the newcomers hastened to introduce themselves to the region's farmers and carpenters. More difficult were the local wives who, distrustful at first, had to be approached with caution. The artists therefore began with the children who were quick to share their hearth-baked crepes, and through this circuitous route they at last won the hearts of the Breton women. Soon they were invited by the villagers to participate in weddings and local *Pardons* (religious festivities), and to linger over mugs of apple brandy.

Marie Pape recalled the late evenings that Gauguin and his friends spent at the Kervastor farm nearby. While they stuffed themselves with grilled chestnuts and buckwheat cakes, the farm's owner filled their heads with legends of the Bois d'Amour. According to legend, on certain winter nights fires break out and seize the hearts of those in love, taking them far away. After one such evening, a hungover Gauguin gravely told Marie "There may very well be evil spirits in those woods. When we left the farm I felt a great chill against my face and then nothing: the evil spirits must have transported me by air." It is more likely that the only spirit that transported him was apple alcohol.

"Only God is Permanent"

André Gide's *If the Seed Lives* gives us an on-the-spot report of the atmosphere which reigned at Pouldu where Gauguin and his followers had migrated in 1889.

"Proceeding in short stages, from Quiberon to Quimper, I followed the coastline until I reached a tiny village, at the end of the day. The village, called Pouldu, consisted of four houses, two of which were inns; the least imposing took my fancy and I entered quite thirsty. A servant led me into a bare whitewashed room whose sparse furnishings made the numerous canvases on its walls all the more noticeable... I contemplated them with growing amazement. It seemed to me that they were only infantile daubings, but in such lively, unusual and joyful tones that I couldn't possibly think of leaving."

Gide watched as Sérusier, Filiger and Gauguin arrived, barefoot, "superbly untidy" and singing opera at the top of their lungs. What a strange encounter between the future author of the *Nourishing Earth* ("Tell yourself, Nathaniel, that only God is permanent... That the importance should be in your way of seeing and not in the thing being seen.") and the singers of the newborn School of Pouldu!

Praising Gauguin in the *Mercure de France* of March 1891, the art critic Aurier defined Symbolism as follows: "A work of art should be 1) idealist, since its unique ideal will be the expression of an idea; 2) symbolist, since it expresses that idea in forms; 3) synthetic, because the object will only be considered as a sign of the perceived idea; 4) decorative..." If, according to Maurice Denis, Gauguin was not a "teacher" but "an intuitive", he "was, all the same, the uncontested master whose talent, facility, gesture, physical force, inexhaustive imagination, resistance to alcohol and romanticism one greatly admires."

Gauguin was certainly the violent catalyst and leader of the aesthetic and moral movement that was born at Pont-Aven and developed at Pouldu. Taking its sources from Breton folk art, the English Pre-Raphaelites, Japanese prints and literary symbolism, this movement ironically labeled itself as both 'Impressionist' and 'Synthetic' at its first exhibition at the Volponi Café in 1889. However, Gauguin was also a bit of a spoilsport, going off to play elsewhere when things weren't as he wanted them to be. His disappearance to the Pacific caused the disbanding of the group. He took away with him in his knapsack their 'enthusiasm', the 'divine transport' and the 'sacred madness', leaving them with only a memory, when phantom freighters passed in the distance.

Paul Gauguin: **Bonjour, Monsieur Gauguin** (1889).

Camille Pissarro: Charcoal Portrait of Gauguin.

Two Breton women at a gate (photo).

Paul Gauguin: **The David Mill at Pont–Aven** (1894).

Carpenters at Pont–Aven (photo).

Laundresses at Pont–Aven (photo).

In constrast with **Bonjour, Monsieur Courbet,** this **Bonjour, Monsieur Gauguin** shows a more grimly introspective author pausing in peasant's sabots before a gate. The woman about to open the gate is seen against a wintry landscape whose bared branches remind us of the outlining in Gothic stained glass windows.

Gauguin surrendered himself to the Celtic soul of the Breton landscape whose meandering rivers and old mills became immortalized in his paintings. The boldness and extravagance displayed in these paintings were criticized by Pissarro and Cézanne.

The old rue de Concarneau at Pont-Aven.

Emile Jourdan: **Rue de Concarneau.**

Rue de Concarneau on Fair Day (photo).

Inhabitants of Pont-Aven (photo).

From the moment of his arrival in Pont-Aven, in June 1886, Paul Gauguin was touched by the adventurous spirit and playful character of the inhabitants of this village. Although Pont-Aven's popularity with writers and artists dated back to the 1860's, at the time of Gauguin's arrival, it was still relatively unspoiled. Gauguin went to stay at the family pension run by Marie-Jeanne Gloanec, whom Émile Jourdan described as a "real mother for artists." Posing with her guests, including Gauguin (seated in the foreground), Madame Gloanec seems to back up Jourdan's statement.

While staying at this pension Gauguin wrote to his abandoned wife: "I am working a lot and with great success... everyone argues about my advice."

Paul Gauguin: **Ham** (1889).

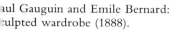
Paul Gauguin and Emile Bernard:
Sculpted wardrobe (1888).

The Gloanec Pension (photo with Gauguin in the foreground).

Gauguin painted many still lifes based on the table settings at the Gloanec Pension. One of these, the **White Table Cloth,** still bears traces of his former association with the Impressionists.

Émile Bernard was recommended to Gauguin by Émile Schuffenecker. After crossing all of Brittany on foot, Bernard met up with Gauguin and came to admire him greatly. In the summer of 1888 they collaborated in carving a cupboard.

Along with Laval, Meyer de Haan, Jourdan, Moret and Sérusier, they formed a noisy and rowdy group. They called themselves 'Impressionists' as opposed to 'Academicists' whom they mocked.

Paul Gauguin: **White Tablecloth "Pension Gloanec"** (1886).

Emile Bernard: **Yellow Tree** (1888).

Young girls in the Bois d'Amour (photo).

O n a beautiful sunny day in October 1888, Gauguin led Sérusier into the Bois d'Amour and gave him a painting lesson. Sérusier began painting a landscape on a cigar box lid and was stopped by Gauguin after having painted only a few dominant colors. The lesson went as follows: "How do you see that tree? It's yellow? Well, then put down yellow. And that shade is rather blue. So render it with pure ultramarine. And those leaves—red aren't they? Use vermillion." And so synthesist painting was born. Returning to Paris, Sérusier showed his revolutionary sketch, **The Talisman,** to his fellow students at the Academy Jullian. They were staggered by this almost abstract painting which was "so synthetically formulated as to be formless." Bernard's **Yellow Tree** is a perfect example of this new way of depicting reality. Maurice Denis will remember Gauguin's lesson when catching his **Sun Spots** and remind anyone listening that "A picture, before being a war horse or a nude or some anecdotal scene, is essentially a flat surface covered with colors arranged in a certain order." Although they came very close to abstraction, they were nevertheless afraid to go further and their art remained in a figurative mode.

Maurice Denis: **Splashes of Sunlight on a Terrace** (October 1890).

194

Paul Sérusier: **The Talisman** (October 188

Emile Bernard: **Breton Women in a Field** (1888).

Paul Gauguin: **The Belle Angèle** (1889)

Breton women fording the river Aven (photo).

Photographic portrait
of Angèle Satre.

Vincent Van Gogh: **Ballroom at the Folies Arlésiennes** (1888).

I
n October 1888, Gauguin
descended to the south of France
where he joined up with Vincent
Van Gogh at Arles.

Gauguin brought a canvas of
Bernard's with him which was
"cloisonné like a stained glass
window." The flat, boldly outlined
forms of Bernard's **Breton Women
in a Field** can also be seen in
Gauguin's own **Vision After the
Sermon.** Excited by this painting,
Van Gogh followed suit with
**Ballroom at the Folies
Arlésiennes.**

Soon a painterly dialogue was
established between these two artists.
They painted the inhabitants and cafés
at Arles and argued over the light and
its colors. Frustrated, furious and mad
with despair, Vincent attempted to kill
Gauguin; then he cut off his own ear.
The distraught Gauguin fled to
Brittany where he was commissioned to
paint a portrait of the wife of the future
mayor of Pont-Aven. Despite its
daring composition, this Symbolist
portrait of **The Belle Angèle** (Satre)
was not at all pleasing to the mayor.

Photographic portrait of
an old woman from Arles.

Vincent Van Gogh:
Old Arlesian Woman.

Paul Sérusier: **Solitude.**

Jan Verkade:
Breton Woman (1892).

Young girls in the Bois d'Amour (photo).

Little Breton girl
on the rocks in
the Bois d'Amour (photo).

Pierre Puvis de Chavannes:
**Young Women at
the Seashore** (1879).

198

Emile Bernard: **Madeleine in the Bois d'Amour** (1888).

The Bois d'Amour (Wood of Love) at Pont-Aven lived up to its name which was derived from the lovemaking that took place near its river banks. It was a favorite spot for the young Breton women who spent idle moments daydreaming in the magical woods. Full of romantic thoughts they remind us of Puvis de Chavannes' **Young girls at the Sea.** His allegorical friezes and mystical settings were remembered by the painters at Pont-Aven and Pouldu. Émile Bernard portrayed his cherished sister in the painting **Madeleine in the Bois d'Amour.**

Verkade recognized his indebtedness to Gauguin in the realization that his spirit was "the principle which organizes everything nature has to offer," yet he eventually gave up painting and entered a monastery. In the meantime, Gauguin, the new master of symbolism, decided to escape by sea to a free world of absolute pleasure.

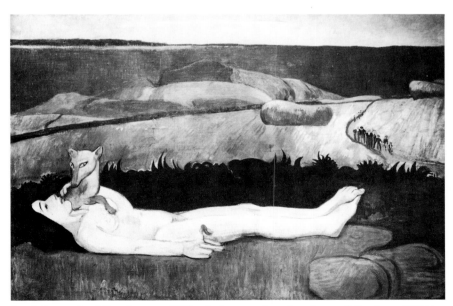

Paul Gauguin: **The Loss of Virginity or Awakening of Spring** (1891).

Paul Gauguin: **The Green Christ** (1899).

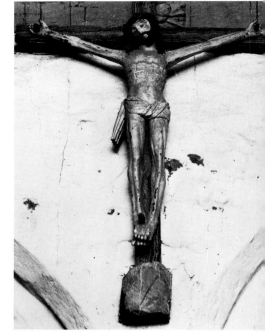

The polychrome wooden Crucifix from the Tremalo Chapel (photo).

Gauguin took the same yellow Christ out of the lonely chapel at Tremalo, planted it in the middle of a wheatfield and surrounded it with praying figures. Likewise, he moved the granite crucifix, green with age, from the church yard at Nizon. He chose the detail of the descent from the cross and added a stormy horizon beyond the rose-colored dunes of Pouldu.

Filiger came even closer to the naivety of Breton sculpture in his painting of the same Tremalo Christ, replacing Gauguin's praying figures with grazing animals. For both Gauguin and Filiger it was a matter of sacrificing everything for art. Gauguin shows this in **Christ in the Olive Grove** where he depicted his own features on Christ's face.

The Calvary from Nizon (photo).

Charles Filiger: **Christ at Landes.**

Paul Gauguin: **The Yellow Christ** (1889).

The 1889 World's Fair on the Champs-de-Mars.

EXPOSANTS

Paul Gauguin   E. Schuffenecker   Emile Bernard
Charles Laval   Louis Anquetin   Louis Roy
Léon Fauché   Georges Daniel   Ludovic Nemo

List of exhibitors in Synthesists exhibition. Engraving by Gauguin.

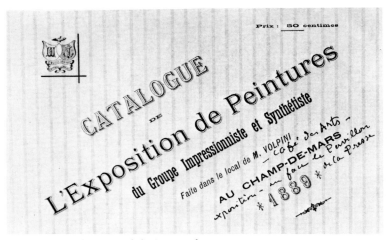

Cover of Synthesists exhibition catalogue.

Emile Bernard: **Nightmare** (1889).

Disappointed at not being able to participate in the Fine Arts Exhibition at the 1889 World's Fair, Gauguin leaped at Emile Schuffenecker's idea of organizing their own exhibition at the Café Volponi situated next to the Press Pavilion on the fairground.

Replacing the café's mirrors with their own paintings, this impromptu group of "Synthesists"—who still didn't dare to completely renounce the name "Impressionist"—showed their work in the Bohemian atmosphere of the café. It was a failure. No sales and no praise—except for the critic Aurier who mentioned that "in these days of excessive cleverness and faking" it was interesting to see "research into the simplification of means."

Still, the exhibition at the Italian Volponi's café was a revelation for the young painters from the Academy Jullian who, along with Maurice Denis, recognized Gauguin as their "uncontested chief" and founded the group called the Nabis.

Emile Bernard: **Dreaming**
(illustration for catalogue).

Paul Gauguin: **The Schuffenecker Family** (1889).

Paul Gauguin: **Hay Makers**
(illustration for exhibition catalogue).

Emile Schuffenecker: **Women Gathering Seaweed.**

The Inn of Marie Henry, called Marie Poupée. Pouldu (photo).

Dining room wall mural by Gauguin and Meyer de Haan (photo).

The Grands Sables beach at Pouldu.

Jacob Meyer de Haan: **Women Grinding Hemp** (1889)

Charles Filiger:
Landscape at Pouldu
(c. 1897).

204

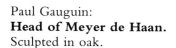

Paul Gauguin:
Head of Meyer de Haan.
Sculpted in oak.

Jacob Meyer de Haan: **Motherhood, Marie Henry Feeding Her Child** (c. 1891).

Toward the end of September 1889, fleeing from the hordes of tourists and painters at Pont-Aven, Gauguin and Sérusier emigrated to Pouldu further up the coast of Brittany. They installed themselves at the small inn, run by Marie Henry, near the Great Sands beach. Meyer de Haan joined them and won the tender heart of their hostess, who was nicknamed Marie Poupée ('Doll') because of her beauty. Above is a portrait that De Haan painted of her feeding their child. This touching portrayal of maternity will be referred to later by Maurice Denis when he painted his own wife and child. Filiger, Laval, Moret and Maufra soon arrived at Pouldu and these artists became so involved in Synthesist painting that it seems more appropriate to speak in terms of a Pouldu School rather than a Pont-Aven School. The walls of Marie Henry's inn were soon covered with their paintings, some of which are reproduced here: **Women Grinding Hemp** between the **Swan** and **Breton Joan of Arc** by Gauguin. Not limiting himself to painting, Gauguin sculpted a bust of Meyer de Haan which was placed on the inn's mantlepiece.

Maurice Denis:
Mother and Child
(1895).

Paul Sérusier: **Pont-Aven Triptych** (1891).

Paul Sérusier's allegorical **Pont-Aven Triptych** *refers to the happiness of sharing the fruits of th[e] Tree of Beauty with companions. Sérusier combined elements taken from both Puvis de Chavanne[s] and local folk art, and incorporated them into his own squat, condensed and introspective style. Se[e]*

against a sky, colored green as a symbol of hope, the tree is outlined by the navy blue of the Great Sands cove.

Gauguin would refer to this painting six years later, when he worked on his famous Tahitian painting entitled **Where do we come from? Where are we? Where are we going?**

Paul Gauguin: **Breton Landscape with a Dog** (1889).

Little girl from Douëlen (photo).

Charles Filiger:
**Young Breton
Fisherman.**

Paul Gauguin: **The House of the Hanged Man** (1889).

Charles Filiger: **House of the Hanged Man I** (Allegorical Landscape).

Pouldu's coastal setting was soon transformed on the artists' canvases. The fleeting sunlight on its hillsides and cottages, the little girls gathering flowers, the rugged rocks and lone lighthouses were just a few of the subjects these artists converted into Symbolist canvases. An isolated house looking out over the sea at Penmarch Point attracted both Gauguin and Filiger, whose different versions offer an interesting contrast. Whereas Gauguin's is full of pastoral charm, Filiger's is more impressive in its daring structure and delicate outlines. Antoine de La Rouchefoucauld, Filiger's patron and friend, wrote in 1893: "It is a miracle to see this inspired illuminator interpret nature... The **House of the Hanged Man** is one of the most curious landscapes to this day. It is intense, distressing and filled with unlimited pity."

Another fervent admirer was the novelist Alfred Jarry who called Filiger a "transformer." Perhaps it would make sense to say that he was in fact the most secret "reformer" of the Pouldu artists.

House above the Grand Sables beach at Pouldu (photo).

Young Breton women at the Kersellec well (photo).

Jacob Meyer de Haan: **Farm with Wells, Pouldu.** Kersellec (1889).

Henry Moret: **The Island of Houat** (1893).

Photographic portrait of Kersellec farmer.

The writer François Ménez describes Brittany: "La Cornouaille, spread out in all its magnitude is best characterized by the flow of light and color. It is covered, according to season, in gold and violet scarves of wildflowers and heather. Its forests guard the secrets of forgotten fairies and enchanters under its foliage…"

Gustave Flaubert, despite his Norman roots, was also captivated by Brittany. In his Through fields and shores he described the discoveries he made while traveling there. Gauguin's disciples restored the symbolic value to color by attributing to it a profound force, linking it with the very soul of the countryside. Color now had a depth that was echoed and illuminated by their landscapes

Paul Gauguin: **The Gate** (1889).

Breton pig raisers (photo).

Cuno Amiet: **Violet Calf in a Field** (1896).

211

Henry Moret: **Rolling at Pouldu** (1894).

Working the Fields in Brittany (photo).

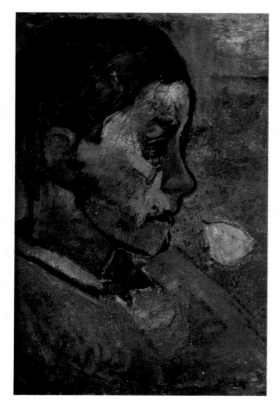

Wladysla Slewinski:
Boy with Red Flower
(c. 1898).

Nothing of that varied Breton landscape escaped
these artists. They depicted its rickety gates
and lopsided farms, its pastures, and those
who tilled the earth. They took this earth and nourished
it with bold colors. They followed the animals and their
guardians.

Their's was a love story, with all its attachments,
excesses and destruction. Gauguin crossed this
countryside like a meteorite leaving golden works in his
trail.

Paul Sérusier: **Laundresses at Bellangenet** (1892).

Filiger's house at Lannmarch (photo).

Paul Sérusier: **Filiger's House at Lannmarch** (1890).

213

Saint-Maudet Chapel at Pouldu (photo).

Statutes in polychrome wood. Right: Saint-Maudet.

Charles Filiger:
Heads of Young Breton Boys (1890).

Charles Filiger: **Christ and Angels** (1892).

214

Charles Filiger: **Young Breton Cowherder.**

Charles Filiger: **Fisherman's Family** (1894).

Charles Filiger: **Wandering Jew.**

Charles Filiger was one of the Pouldu painters who most frequently referred to the medieval art of Breton statuary, found at the nearby chapel of Saint Maudet.

"I paint in secret, in the way that the early Christians prayed," confided Charles Filiger. Fascinated by the dreamy and nostalgic faces of the young fishermen and cow herders, Filiger turned them into primitive and Byzantine angels. These "mystical and sensual adolescent profiles" (as described by Jarry) take on an almost sacred quality.

Filiger was gravely neurotic and as solitary as the **Wandering Jew** with whom he compared himself. He sought but never found happiness in his renditions of beautiful young men.

Paul Sérusier: **Paul Gauguin Playing the Accordian** (1890).

Breton's dancing (photo).

Festivities at Pont-Aven (photo).

Paul Gauguin: **Breton Girls** (1886).

Although Gauguin's **Breton Girls,** *painted at Pont-Aven in 1886, bears traces of Pissarro's influence, he developed his own style upon moving to Pouldu*

At Pouldu he became more directly involved in village life. Paul Sérusier's sketch of him playing the accordian testifies to his participation in local activities. It was at Pouldu that Gauguin's influence on his comrades was most pronounced, as can be seen in the two following examples. In Willumsen's **Brittany,** *Breton women in billowing skirts merrily run to retrieve their husbands from the pub. This painting conveys the condensation and stylization of forms that were particular to this new "naive" art. The featureless and decorative forms of the participants in Maurice Denis'* **Guidel Pardon** *demonstratate his dictum that "above all a painting must decorate". This was the approach adopted also, at a later date, by the Nabis.*

Maurice Denis: **The Guidel Pardon.**

Breton wedding at Pouldu (photo).

Jens Ferdinand Willumsen:
Brittany (1890).

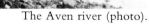

Paul Gauguin:
Aïta Aramoe.
(Pastel dedicated to
his friend Maufra
"artist of the Avant-garde."

Maxime Maufra: **Pont-Aven Landscape.**

A lthough quite
independent, Maxime
Maufra did not altogether
escape from the schematic tendencies
of his much-admired friend,
Gauguin. He did however go
further than Gauguin in his
experiments with the chromatic
combinations of seascapes. In his
Landscape at Pont-Aven,
Maufra perfected the watery green
and blue harmonies of that peaceful
estuary, punctuated with orange fire
and hillside bushes.

While Verkade and Filiger posed
their young Breton swimmers like
Greek gods, Maurice Denis became
preoccupied with the plunging effect
and graphism of Japanese prints.
And so he plunges us into his
Regattas at a Breton port,
where the water gleams and the
winds blow, while Breton women
keep watch over the joyful
swimmers.

Charles Filiger:
Young Bretons at the Sea.

The Aven river (photo).

Jan Verkade: **Young Breton Boy on the Beach.**

Maurice Denis: **Regattas in Breton Port** (1892).

6
THE HILL OF MONTMARTRE AND MONTPARNASSE
Painting Reaches its Zenith

Pablo Picasso: **Self Portrait** (1906).

$\mathbf{I}$N 1907, PICASSO'S *DEMOISELLES d'Avignon,* the painting that stands at the gateway to Cubism, shook not only the official art world, but shocked even his closest friends and supporters. In the *Century of Picasso* Pierre Cabanne tells us that "Derain spread the word around Montmartre that Picasso's canvas was an exercise in despair, and that one day Picasso would be found hanging behind it."

It is essential to understand the origins of that revolt described by Robert Maillard in the *Universal Dictionary of Painting* as "the greatest change in the history of painting since the Renaissance which opened up and influenced many subsequent movements in 20th century painting." Numerous painters accompanied Picasso to Montmartre and later, Montparnasse. The artists who followed or copied this movement were stimulated by its irresistible questioning and geometrical conversion of forms, derived from Cézanne's observation that "all nature is modeled on the sphere, the cone and the cylinder."

Picasso said, "One always speaks of the influence of African art on my work. What can I say? We all love fetishes. Van Gogh said that Japanese art is something they all had in common. For us, it was African art... When I went to the museum at Trocadero it was verminous and moth-eaten. The walls were covered with turkey twill. I was alone. I wanted to leave, but didn't. I understood that it was very important. Something happened to me. The masks weren't sculpture like the others. Not at all—they were magical things... The Africans were intermediaries... Against everything, against unknown spirits, menaces. I looked at the fetishes for quite some time. I understood. I too am against everything. I too think that everything that is unknown is the enemy...! All the fetishes were weapons. To help the people to overcome the power of the evil spirits, to help them become independent... tools. If we give forms to the spirits we become independent. The spirits, the unconscious; the emotion—it's all the same thing... I understood why I was a painter. Alone in that museum, with the masks, Indian dolls and dusty models—the *Demoiselles d'Avignon* should have arrived that day; but not because of the forms: rather because it was my first canvas of exorcism—yes!"

And thus the last word—exorcism—was used giving us the key to Picasso's fantasies, metamorphoses and anamorphosis; the conjuring up of the forces of the psyche which would go toward making a painting which is like the reflections in distorted mirrors.

A Mirror Facing Inwards

Attracted by Impressionism and by the mysterious birth of Cubism, artists came to Paris from all over the world—Spain, Russia, Italy, Germany, Holland, the United States and Japan. Gathering together, they concentrated their energies in the miserable studios of the *Bateau Lavoir* (The Wash House) or the *Ruche* (The Beehive), or in the nearby solitary streets. The cafés and brasseries served as oases when they ran out of paint or were simply overcome by homesickness. These young creators were anxious to express themselves, exchange ideas and change the world by transforming art. And in doing so they made art look back into itself like a inverted mirror—the exterior towards the interior. The outward looking art of their Realist, Impressionist, Divisionist, Symbolist, Fauve or Nabis predecessors gave way to the inward looking visions of Cubism, Futurism, Abstraction and Surrealism.

Turning from objectivity to subjectivity, these artists no longer described—they examined, questioned and interpreted. They deciphered with grids, invented according to their agreed-upon beliefs that were formed on the terraces of brasseries and cafés. In these modern sanctuaries, the spoken word liberated art.

At the same time Freud's analysis of dreams and the libido was being revealed. People began reading his works on the misunderstood role of the unconscious on motivations and contradictions, as well as his writings on guilt, incoherence and aggression. Concurrently, in Europe, there was the acceleration of mechanization and urbanization. There was also the building up of nationalist economic rivalry which helped lead to one of the most terrible confrontations between brother countries—the First World War. And finally, one of the most decisive social revolutions was being fermented—Soviet communism—by men like Lenin and Trotsky at the same cafés and brasseries. As André Malraux noted, "In any case, the transforming power of man began by rebuilding the world and ended by questioning his role." Isn't it in a work of art that man most clearly questions himself? For example, Giorgio de Chirico's prophetic portrait of Guillaume Apollinaire, and all the other canvases or poems that appear premonitory after the fact.

All of these artists, coming from many different countries and backgrounds, having varied personalities and temperaments, took refuge at the heart of Babel which was Montmartre with Montparnasse at the crossroads. Although their works often conflicted, the secrets of their metier revealed the same motto: Art is found in oneself.

"It isn't me who paints, it's my hand guided by my late wife," said Douanier Rousseau. And Picasso, who held an untiring admiration for Rousseau, said, "I paint the things not as I see them, but as I think them to be." Braque, surprised by the "intuitions which distance me more and more from the model," affirmed that there was no certainty except in that which is conceived. For Léger who fitted and welded his ideas together like a genius plumber conquering space, "only the manner in which one treats the subjects is of interest." Modigliani, the incurable romantic, set himself the "real task" of protecting his dreams to such an extent that his models were blinded by them. Soutine became mad while identifying himself with Rembrandt whose introspective gaze appeared to have exhausted the mysteries of the soul. And finally, there was Chagall who envied the kerosene lamp that consumed itself on his table: "It burns away so easily because it drinks its own kerosene to quench its thirst."

There is Nothing Real Apart from Us

For Juan Gris, the most methodically conceptual of all the Cubists, "the world from which I draw the elements is imaginary, not visual... To paint is to *fore-see,* to foresee what is going to happen to the canvas as a whole by introducing a particular form or color and to foresee what sort of reality it might suggest to those who look at it." And from this he concluded, "It is therefore by being my own spectator that I bring out the subject of my canvas." Metzinger and Gleizes agreed in their book *Cubism* that a general and collective vision is impossible: "There is nothing real outside of us. There is nothing real except the coincidence of a sensation and an individual mental direction... rationally we can't ever be certain of the image produced by our senses." And from the Futurist side, Severini announced that "From now on in this time of dynamism and simultaniety, one can only separate reality from memory... by the expanding action which that reality simultaneously evokes within us." Therefore to Descartes', "I think, therefore I am" they have added "I paint, therefore I exist."

Robert Delaunay's 'non-figurative' paintings were creations where colors were to act upon each other "in simultaneous contrasts" building up form and movement in space. Having shaken the *Eiffel Tower* as if under the effect of an earthquake, he stated that "Color is form and subject; it is the only theme that develops, transforms itself apart from all analysis, psychological or otherwise. Color is a function in itself." And even de Chirico, who turned the Montparnasse train station into a dreamlike palace, was absolutely convinced that one only sees things clearly when one's eyes are closed. De Chirico led art toward what he and Apollinaire called "metaphysical painting." After all, isn't Surrealism (whose grandfather was Douanier Rousseau and whose leading practioners included Dali and Delvaux) a metaphorical transfiguration, liberating man from the control of reason, in order to project him into an interspatial universe of dream?

"In order for a work of art to be really immortal it must go completely outside of human limits," thought de Chirico. Matisse said the same thing in different words: "Modern art is an art of invention. It began as an outburst of the heart. It is therefore, by its own essence, closer to the archaic and primitive than to the Renaissance."

To take up Matisse's comparison, it seems true that the important events that took place at Montmartre and Montparnasse from 1907 to 1914 were the result of an international awareness of the values of a personal and collective commitment. This sort of commitment was similar to that which had existed in art before the Renaissance and which was being continued in the tribal arts.

The Artist's Total Commitment

Picasso's experience at the museum at Trocadero and the subsequent catharsis that took place within him, was not such a surprising or unprecedented event. He was not the first to undergo such a cultural shock and create such a commotion as a result.

He was preceded by two great painters whose determining roles have not been sufficiently recognized and whose artistic commitment was total: Paul Gauguin and Douanier Rousseau. Both artists were deeply influenced by primitive art. In Chapter 5 we saw how Gauguin was attracted by the folk art of Brittany and later spent the rest of his life searching for a lost paradise in Oceania. Rousseau was attached to his childhood memories of popular images, frank beliefs and unshakeable spiritualism.

The Spreading of African Rhythm

Picasso's last wife Jacqueline relates how her husband often became seized with a frenzy of creation. He would descend from his studio, enthusiastically crying: "It's coming again. It's coming again"—like an obstetrician announcing the birth of quintuplets.

That happy exclamation can be taken to describe the discoveries made by the artists of Montmartre and Montparnasse where art underwent one of its most productive traumas in man's memory. This was a trauma arising from neither time nor limits. And although there were many artists who felt neglected and isolated themselves in private creativity, this book hopes to show that there were many more who benefited from the confrontations, exchanges and sharing.

We should also recognize that all of these artists had the chance of being aided, stimulated, provoked and proclaimed by a great poet like Apollinaire. For it was he who courageously and eloquently defended Cubism. Apollinaire had the extraordinary gift of omnipresence, a unique intelligence and an innate sense of solidarity.

And, as Valéry said, art is only great when it "commits the entire person." Apollinaire, like Baudelaire, and perhaps even more so, made his life a work of art, an authentic *chef-d'œuvre*.

The commitment of Apollinaire, Picasso and the Cubists, merged together at the accelerated pace of a civilization that had rediscovered African rhythm. "Rhythm is the principle value contributed by Black Africa to the contemporary world. It invades everything—music and dance, of course, but also painting and sculpture," remarked the Senegalese poet Léopold Sedar Senghor.

The **Lapin Agile** (photo).

Rue Saint-Vincent in Montmartre.

André Gill:
Sign for the **Lapin Agile.**

Maurice Utrillo: **The Lapin Agile, Montmartre** (1913).

Père Frédé playing the guitar at the **Lapin Agile.** In the background is Picasso's **Harlequin.**

Pablo Picasso: **Père Frédé.**
Study for **Harlequin with a Glass.**

Pablo Picasso: **Harlequin with a Glass** (1905).

The Lapin Agile ("Agile Rabbit"), at the corner of rue des Saules and rue Saint-Vincent provided cheap meals and entertainment for the artists living in Montmartre. It owed its name to a joke made from the sign post that André Gill had painted showing a rabbit leaping out of a pot, a bottle of wine balanced on its paw. (Le lapin à Gill = the rabbit of Gill).

Its owner not only entertained his customers with his guitar but also served a special cocktail made of cherry liqueur, pernod and grenadine. His special mixture was responsible for his hoarse voice and his acquisition of Picasso's **Harlequin with a Glass.** Picasso was given so many of these cocktails on the house that he

gave Frédé this painting which can be seen hanging in the background in the photograph on the opposite page. This canvas hung next to a Wasley Crucifix and a plaster cast of a Cambodian Khmer statue.

In his self-portrait, Picasso is dressed as a clown and accompanied by his mistress Fernande Olivier. The pouting Fernande wears a Bonnard hat, is silhouetted like a Lautrec and is done in garish colors that only the Fauves could have painted. Picasso seems to be wondering: "Will alcohol help me to escape from this buffoonery? What is the future of painting? Will I be the leader?... That Cambodian statue is really incredible."

227

At the rue Ravignan was situated a ramshackle building whose wooden partitioned studios were inhabited by some of the greatest artists of our century. It was called the Bateau Lavoir ("Wash house") by the artists because its windows were always filled with their clothes, hung out to dry. Pablo Picasso moved there in April 1904 and became involved with one of his neighbors, Fernande Olivier. They soon struck up a friendship with a fellow lodger, Van Dongen, whose daughter called Picasso "Tablo" (In French, tableau means "painting").

Clovis Sagot introduced Picasso to Gertrude Stein, a wealthy American art collector. The result of this meeting was her portrait. Although Gertrude Stein actually posed for 80 sessions in a broken chair, Picasso, in the end, succeeded in capturing her strong and concentrated face when she was not present. The broken, sculptural style in which he rendered her features hints at the coming explosion of Cubism.

The **Bateau Lavoir** at place Émile-Goudeau (photo).

Photographic portrait of Gertrude Stein.

Pablo Picasso: **Gertrude Stein** (1906).

Photograph of Fernande Olivier and Pablo Picasso.

Photograph of Fernande Olivier and Dolly Van Dongen.

Kees Van Dongen: **The Belle Fernande** (1906).

Photograph of Van Dongen with his daughter Dolly.

André Warnod: **Entrance to the Bateau Lavoir.**

The **Bateau Lavoir** at night (photo).

Posted on Picasso's door was the notice "The Poets' Rendez-vous." Among the "poets" who visited this studio were Max Jacob, Guillaume Apollinaire, André Salmon, Kees Van Dongen, Juan Gris, Marie Laurencin, Georges Braque, André Derain, and Maurice Vlaminck. Art lovers such as Gertrude Stein and her brother Michael, Wilhelm Uhde and Daniel Kahnweiler also gathered here. "Picasso's crew" moved about from cabaret to restaurant, enlarging its numbers along the way. They often held impromptu dinners at the Bateau Lavoir, prolonging their aesthetic debates by drinking and smoking a bit of opium.

Photograph of the **Bateau Lavoir** with Picasso's comments: "Window of my studio at 13 rue Ravignan."

The Place Ravignan (postcard).

230

Juan Gris: **Place Ravignan.**

Hearing of his fellow countryman's reputation, Juan Gris came to Paris from Madrid in 1906 and installed himself at the Bateau Lavoir. Although he stayed there until 1922, he did not really become interested in Cubism until after Picasso's departure in 1912 to larger quarters at 11 Blvd Clichy. For Gris, Cubism was more than just a technique, it was a demanding and moral "state of spirit." His visions were above all "conceptual," as is proved by comparing his **Figure of a Woman** with the photograph of his companion Josette. "Cézanne turned a bottle into a cylinder, I turn a cylinder into a bottle." He methodically sought the principles of an "essential and integral architecture" which could embrace the world. He honored Picasso in his remarkable portrait which was shown at the Salon des Indépendants in 1912.

Juan Gris: **Woman.**

Photograph of Juan Gris and his wife in his studio at the **Bateau Lavoir.**

The poet Max Jacob called the Bateau Lavoir *the "The Laboratory of Art";* however, the name *"Cradle of Cubism" is equally fitting. If Cézanne was the grandfather of* **The Demoiselles d'Avignon,** *the "quintuplets," no one can doubt Picasso's paternity.*

At the suggestion of Apollinaire, Georges Braque studied these five sisters, but was terrified by their disjointedness. "Listen" he told Picasso, "it's as if you want us to drink gasoline in order to spit on a fire." But Picasso continued to give 'sisters' to **The Demoiselles d'Avignon** *and Braque overcame his fears and presented them with a 'cousin': his large* **Standing Nude.**

Pablo Picasso: **Nude Against a Red Background** (1906).

Georges Braque: **Standing Nude.**

Photograph of Picasso at the **Bateau Lavoir.**

Photograph of Braque in his studio.

Juan Gris: **Homage to Pablo Picasso** (1912).

232

Paul Cézanne: **Three Bathers** (1879–82).

Pablo Picasso: **Demoiselles d'Avignon** (1907).

Picasso's **Demoiselles d'Avignon** *not only stands as a revolutionary statement but it shows as well the artist's enormous capacity for assimilation. Critics speak of the influences of African art, of an Iberian heritage and Egyptian ascendancy... Douanier Rousseau remarked to Picasso, "We are both the greatest painters of our time. You in the Egyptian style and myself in the modern." First titled the* **Proof of Sin,** *the* **Demoiselles** *owe their Egyptian blood to the low relief sculptures at the Louvre, and their Asian blood to the Khmer statue at the Lapin Agile. Their African treatment borrows from the masks at the museum at Trocadero as well from as those collected by Matisse, Derain and Vlaminck. The primitive aspect comes from Gauguin, the revolutionary tone from Manet and Lautrec and the naiveté from Douanier Rousseau.*

Maurice de Vlaminck: **Bathers** (1906–07).

Scene of Egyptian banquet (18th dynasty).

Gabon mask belonging to Vlaminck and Derain.

John the Baptist in the Desert, 8th century (Museum of Catalonia, Barcelona).

Regardless of interceptions or intercessions in **Demoiselles d'Avignon** *(in fact the name is "d'Avigno"—the name of a street in the red light district of Barcelona), Picasso's scandalous canvas was for him, "my first canvas of exorcism." It was the equivalent of Courbet's* **Bonjour, Monsieur Courbet** *and Manet's* **Déjeuner sur l'herbe.** *From the latter painting, Picasso derived his nude seated at the right, head in hands with ironic eye and the still life on the cloth.*

Evidence of Gauguin's **Vision after the Sermon** *and Henri Rousseau's* **War** *is also found in Picasso's work.*

And so Picasso's painting was a dramatic catharsis—comparable also to the **Salon de la rue des Moulins** *for Lautrec—which enabled him to reject the emotional hold of his mother (from whom he borrowed his pseudonym Picasso), and that of his overbearing father (who made him draw pigeon's feet until he had them perfect). It also marked his liberation from the influences of Cézanne and Lautrec, whom he felt he had to surpass and outclass.*

The miracle was an intimate eruption that came out of the deep need of the times. Picasso said, "A painting is the best hidden image of the one who paints it."

Pablo Picasso: **Study for Demoiselles d'Avignon** (1907).

Nigerian wooden mask.

Pablo Picasso: **Study for the Demoiselles d'Avignon** (1907).

Mrs. Van Dongen and her daughter in front of **Demoiselles d'Avignon** at the **Bateau Lavoir** (1907).

234

Pablo Picasso: **Demoiselles d'Avignon** (1907).

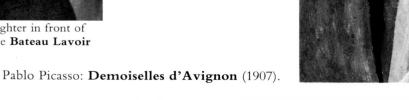

Photographic portrait
of Guillaume Apollinaire.

Photographic portrait of Marie Laurencin.

Max Jacob and Pablo Picasso
at Montmartre (photo).

Marie Laurencin: **Group of Artists** (1908).

Henri Rousseau: **Portrait of Guillaume Apollinaire and Marie Laurencin** (1909).

Henri Rousseau: **Portrait of a Woman.**

We are united to celebrate your glory. Let's drink these wines poured by Picasso. For this is the time to drink to them crying in unison: Long live Rousseau!"

This spirited toast was made during a banquet held in honor of Douanier Rousseau at the Bateau Lavoir in November 1908. The above toast was written by Apollinaire who had introduced Rousseau to Picasso. Picasso had just bought Rousseau's immense **Portrait of a Woman** which he had fallen in love with at first sight.

Delighted by all this attention, Rousseau thought of a portrait that he would do of Apollinaire and his 'Muse', Marie Laurencin. He depicted Apollinaire as "large" because he was "a great poet." Although Rousseau was often misunderstood and mocked by his contemporaries, certain faithful friends, such as Apollinaire, appreciated his work. Apollinaire was able to look beyond the naïveté of Rousseau's work and find in it a profound vision of the future.

Pablo Picasso: **Portrait of Max Jacob.**

André Salmon in Picasso's studio at the **Bateau Lavoir** (photo 1908).

The rue de l'Abreuvoir in Montmartre (photo).

Pablo Picasso: **The Sacré-Cœur** (1909).

At the time when artists began to make their slow descent from the Butte of Montmartre toward Montparnasse, the last bits of scaffolding were being taken down from the Basilica of the Sacred Heart. This new cathedral, designed by Abadie, was an ideal subject for painters. Its erect cones and massive white marble surfaces were especially interesting to the early analytic Cubists.

It was during this time that the friendship and interchange of ideas between Picasso and Braque were fortified. Together, they took up where Cézanne had left off in a "plastic reconversion based on structure and rhythm."

Construction of the Sacred Heart Cathedral in Montmartre (photo).

Georges Braque: **The Sacré-Cœur in Montmartre** (1910).

Maurice Utrillo: **Rue Chappe** (c. 1912).

Suzanne Valadon also played with the rhythms created by the trees and rooftops climbing toward the opaque dome of the Basilica of the Sacred Heart. Her son Utrillo joined her in their garden at the rue Cortot and produced his own version of one of the most celebrated landmarks of Paris. Valadon admired the sensitive understanding of tone evidenced in her son's painting, saying with characteristic sincerity, "I am jealous of his feeling for purity, lightness and fluidity." Utrillo, using his photographic memory and picture postcards, achieved this fluidity by working at incredible speed.

The Sacred Heart Cathedral in Montmartre (photo).

Suzanne Valadon: **Sacré-Cœur Seen from the Garden at rue Cortot** (1916).

Amedeo Modigliani:
**Portrait of
Paul Guillaume.**

Photograph of Daniel
Kahnweiler taken by Picasso
in his studio at Blvd. de
Clichy.

Photographic portrait
of Wilhelm Uhde.

Kees Van Dongen: **Portrait of Kahnweiler** (1907).

Pablo Picasso: **Portrait of Daniel Kahnweiler** (1910).

Robert Delaunay: **Portrait of Wilhelm Uhde** (1907).

Pablo Picasso: **Portrait of Wilhelm Uhde** (1910).

240

Photograph of
Ambroise Vollard (1899).

Paul Cézanne: **Portrait of Ambroise Vollard** (1899).

Pablo Picasso: **Ambroise Vollard** (1909–1910).

The portraits on these two pages are
dedicated to the critics, dealers and
collectors whose ability to understand the
artists' efforts was of paramount importance to the
development of modern art. These men and
women included Vollard, who exhibited Cézanne
and early Picasso; Gertrude and Michael Stein, at
whose home Picasso and Matisse met and sized
each other up; Uhde, whose painter wife, Sonia,
teamed up with Robert Delaunay; Paul
Guillaume who encouraged Modigliani, and
Daniel Kahnweiler, who was stunned by the
daring of **Demoiselles d'Avignon.**

Matisse painting Michael Stein's portrait (photo).

241

Soda siphons, liqueur bottles, newspapers and cigarettes replaced vases of flowers and bowls of fruit as the subjects of Cubist still lifes.

From the terraces at the Rotunde or Dome brasseries, which face each other across the Boulevard Montparnasse, Picasso, Braque and their fellow painters found contemporary themes for their revolutionary paintings. The oval trays of the waiters and the café tables became still lifes where forms were broken up and intermingled. Objects became fragmented. This fragmentation allowed the object to be seen from various viewpoints and angles. These experiments with a new visual approach encouraged the spectator to look under, over and inside objects—to explore them. As Braque said, he wanted "not just to see but to hold things."

Georges Braque: **Side Table or Bottle and Newspaper** (1911).

Montparnasse barman (photo).

Jean Cocteau: **The Rotonde in 1915** (left to right: Frère Jean, Kisling, Cocteau, Picasso, Konsky and Pâquerette).

Pablo Picasso: **Bottle of Vieux Marc** (1913).

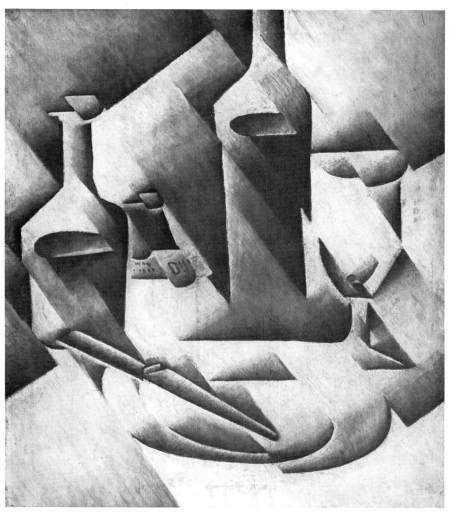

Juan Gris: **Still Life: Bottles and Knife** (1912).

Jean Metzinger: **Still Life with a Pipe** (1913).

Customers on the terrace of the **Rotonde** (1910).

The Montmartre-Saint-Germain-des-Prés bus (photo).

Anton Kaminsky: **Corner of Avenue du Maine and Blvd de Vaugirard.**

Place Rennes and the Montparnasse train station (photo 1900).

Giorgio de Chirico: **Montparnasse Train Station 1914, or Melancholy of Departure.**

Montparnasse became the new crossroads for painters, sculptors and poets. André Warnod called it "The Promised Land, spoken of throughout the world... cafés bustling like train platforms, filled with travelers and emigrants." The Symbolist poet Paul Fort held court at the Closerie des Lilas, where in 1912 he was proclaimed "Prince of Poets." Soon artists and writers who lived in Montmartre began arriving in Montparnasse in buses that brought them from the Butte. Picasso pointed out to Apollinaire the "painter of train stations" —Giorgio de Chirico. Apollinaire summoned up the notion of "metaphysical landscape" in his poem Nights in Paris, after seeing de Chirico's painting. The receding lines and spatial tensions creating the dreamlike atmosphere of de Chirico's work announced the arrival of Surrealism.

André Rouveyre: **Paul Fort.**

Photograph of Paul Fort.

Juan Gris: **Man at a Café** (1912).

André Warnod:
**Guillaume Apollinaire
and Max Jacob in Montparnasse.**

André Lhote: **Poster for the Bal Bullier.**

Entrance to the **Bal Bullier** (photo).

Francis Picabia: **Dance of Spring** (1912).

Sonia Terk Delaunay: **Bal Bullier or Tango at the Bal Bullier** (1913).

246

Across the street from the Closerie des Lilas, *at the border of Montparnasse and the Latin Quarter, was the Bal Bullier. Here a mixture of artists, intellectuals and students made up a cosmopolitan world. Arriving from the nearby Luxembourg Gardens, they were anxious to try out the newly discovered Argentinian tango with its sudden embracing and frenetic momentum.*

At this time, 1912, Braque and Picasso passed from Cubism's 'analytical' to its 'synthetic' phase. This 'synthetic Cubism' attempted to express the reality of an object by the insertion of concrete elements such as pasted papers, fabrics, and lettering. Parallel to this phase, several new aesthetic trends were born. Rejecting static contemplation, these new directions aspired towards movement that would express life's tensions and the vitality of its forms through color. This trend was found in the Italian Severini's Futurism and in the research of Picabia, whose puzzles were "burning works which relate astonishing conflicts between pictorial materials and the imagination."

Sonia and Robert Delaunay's 'orphism' formed an "off-shoot of Cubism" by using "the simultaneous contrast of colors." The supple, fluctuating movement of their rainbow colors is like a swaying waltz or a lanquid tango.

Gino Severini: **Blue Dancer** (1912).

The terrace of the **Closerie des Lilas** (photo).

The Ruche at night (photo).

Fernand Léger: **Woman Sewing** (1909).

The garden at the **Ruche** in 1906 (photo).

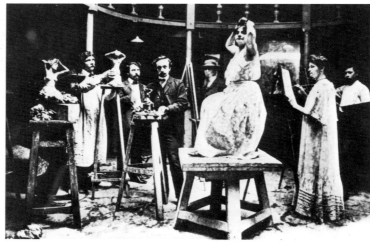

The Academy of the **Ruche** around 1905 (photo).

Photograph of Fernand Léger and his wife Louise in his studio at the **Ruche** around 1910.

A beehive buzzing with activity, the Ruche (The Beehive) at 52 rue Dantzig was to Montparnasse what the Bateau Lavoir was to Montmartre. It was an academy where the greatest masters of the School of Paris were revealed. Renovated from the former Wine Pavilion of the 1900 World's Fair, this building was first inhabited by the sculptor Alfred Boucher who transformed it into a studio. The Ruche housed Léger, Chagall, Modigliani, Soutine, Kisling, Kikoïne, Krémègne, Zadkine and Archipenko. They brought along friends, musicians, poets, fiancées and mistresses.

Sensitive to the syncopated rhythms of mechanical industrialization, Fernand Léger created an art of confrontations and a "battle of volumes" ironically called "tubist." Influenced by Cézanne, Picasso and Douanier Rousseau, Léger became the prophetic painter of civilization. His was a friendly, choreographed universe in which man and robot lived and swam together in space.

Fernand Léger: **Nude in a Forest** (1910–11).

Fernand Léger: **Smoke Over Rooftops** (1912).

Entrance to the **Ruche** (photo).

Marc Chagall: **Self Portrait with Seven Fingers** (1912–13).

Marc Chagall and Bella (photo).

"While an offended model's sobs can be heard coming from the Russian's studio, the Italians try to drown them out with their guitars... and I sit staring at my kerosene lamp," was Chagall's description of the sounds of the Ruche. The wandering creator of **Self portrait with Seven Fingers** dwells on his memories of Russia and of his fiancée Bella, whom he had left behind at Vitebsk. There she is wearing black gloves and sharing Chagall's dreams of those summer nights when apparitions float above the rooftops of Russian villages.

"Time is a river without shores" was Chagall's justification for his timeless images. For him, "art is a state of the soul"—a child's soul, depicting the Eiffel Tower from his window at the Ruche.

A native of Cracow, Moïse Kisling was a tower of strength for his friends. His door and heart were open wide to everyone. Rich and poor, famous and unknown, whether painter, poet, sculptor or eternal student, all felt at home at his studio. He was of particular help to Modigliani, whom he treated as a brother. Kisling's **Self portrait with his wife and dog** shows the artist truly at peace with himself.

Marc Chagall: **My Fiancée in Black Gloves** (1909).

Moïse Kisling in his studio at the **Ruche.**

Moïse Kisling:
Self Portrait with his Wife and Dog Kouski.

251

Photograph of Paul Krémègne.

Paul Krémègne: **Self Portrait.**

Studios at the **Ruche** (photo).

Paul Krémègne: **Mme Oustroun's House at the Ruche.**

Michel Kikoïne: **The Ruche under Snow** (1913-14).

A trio of Lithuanian artists, Paul Krémègne, Michel Kikoïne and Chaïm Soutine—whose friendship dated back to their student days at the School of Fine Arts in Vilnius were reunited at the Ruche. Krémègne and Kikoïne have left us with their portraits of the Ruche as seen in summer and under snow.

Soutine, the most Expressionist of the three, surpassed them with the fantastic originality of his painting. Speaking about his painting of a flayed ox, whose subject he had taken from Rembrandt's painting at the Louvre,

Soutine was reported to have said, "In the body of a woman Courbet was able to express the atmosphere of Paris—I want to show Paris in the carcass of an ox."

Soutine was a visionary trying to transfigure his still lifes to the point of lyrical abstraction. The art historian Elie Faure wrote, "I think of Soutine, drunk and groping, yet one of the most powerful symphonic geniuses who had ever existed, frantic in his colored universe where seemingly choatic forms organize themselves bit by bit into a troubled vision."

Photograph of Michel Kikoïne and his wife.

Michel Kikoïne: **Self Portrait.**

Chaïm Soutine: **Turkey and Tomatoes.**

It's not surprising that an expressionism as violent as this should have broken at the moment when Cubism organized and multiplied with so many chromatic precautions and linear measures. As Elie Faure sensed, it was then that "the imagination of excited people hovered around an invisible flame whose center was Paris, where each of them feverishly tossed about the treasures and scraps of their souls."

Modigliani would one day say of his friend Soutine, "The great rascal of our era. Next to him, I don't exist."

Chaïm Soutine in his studio at the **Ruche.**

Michel Kikoïne: **Portrait of Soutine.**

Photograph of Blaise Cendrars.

Amedeo Modigliani: **Portrait of Blaise Cendrars** (1917).

Marc Chagall: **Homage to Apollinaire** (1911-12).

I f each painter had his own poet (Blaise Cendrars, Max Jacobs, Paul Fort, André Salmon, Pierre Reverdy and Jean Cocteau), there was one poet who had all the painters—Apollinaire.

He was the magician responsible for the most liberating developments in the history of art. He was also the subject of numerous Cubist, Realist and Surrealist homages. The most mysterious portrait of him was Giorgio de Chirico's symbolic premonitory **Portrait of Guillaume Apollinaire.** The artist saw Apollinaire as an Orpheus, charmer of the sacred fish. His eyes are obscured by the "inky shadows of the sun..." In the background is the artist's profile with the temple encircled by a target. Three years after this portrait was done, Apollinaire was shot in that same encircled spot while serving in the infantry during the First World War.

Chagall's **Homage to Apollinaire** is equally mysterious with its united figure of Adam and Eve posed against a clock-face, summoning up associations with the poet's own verses.

Pablo Picasso: **Picasso Toasting Apollinaire**

Robert Delaunay:
**Portrait of the Poet
Guillaume Apollinaire.**
Study (1911–12).

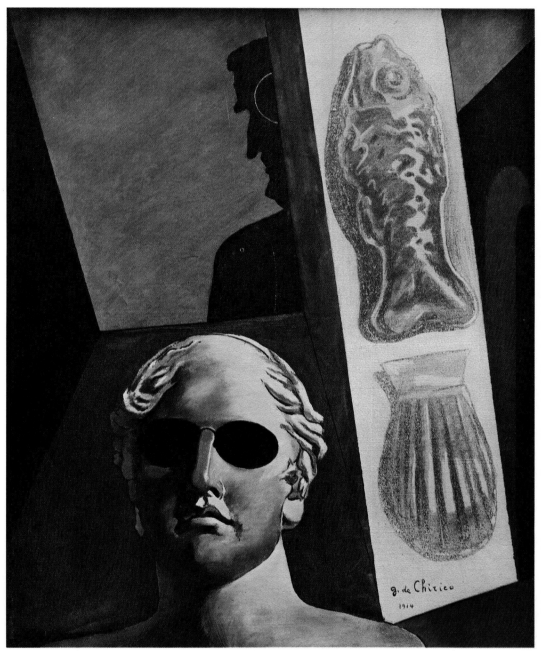

Giorgio De Chirico: **Portrait of Guillaume Apollinaire** (1914).

Photographic portrait of Guillaume Apollinaire.

Louis Marcoussis: **Portrait
of Guillaume Apollinaire** (1912).

Jean Metzinger: **Study for Portrait
of Apollinaire** (1911).

Amedeo Modigliani: **Portrait
of Guillaume Apollinaire** (1917).

255

Kees Van Dongen: **Red Dancer** (1907).

Photograph of Kees Van Dongen
and two models.

Kees Van Dongen moved to
Paris from Holland in 1897.
His early works were
influenced by the Impressionists but he
soon developed his own style. Bold,
broad brush-stokes and heightened
color became his trademark. Women,
particularly nudes, were his favorite
subject. The photograph below shows
one of the many parties that Van
Dongen gave at his studio at Denfert-
Rochereau prior to the First World
War. In the background of the
photograph can be seen the large nudes
and circus paintings for which Van
Dongen was famous.

Costume party at Van Dongen's
studio in 1913 (photo).

Photograph of Foujita on the ocean liner bringing him to France (1913).

Tsuguhara Leonard Foujita: **Nude Combing her Hair.**

Guillaume Apollinaire was heard to complain to his friends at the Café Flore: "Today everything touching upon voluptuousness is surrounded by grandeur and silence. It survives in the sudden and desperate colors of Van Dongen's large figures." Apollinaire regretted that "the austere earnestness of contemporary art has generally banished everything which is seductive and sensuous."

Apollinaire had obviously forgotten two legendary Montparnassian nightowls —Tsuguharu Foujita and Jules Pascin. Pascin's exotic and sophisticated drawings of young girls of the Paris demi-monde hint at both Degas and Toulouse-Lautrec, although they lack the bite of the latter.

And Modigliani? His female nudes are so harmonious and graceful that one doesn't notice that their bodies are often contorted. Although he was aware of Cubist trends, Modigliani painted his in the tradition of Giorgione, Ingres and Manet.

Following pages:
Amedeo Modigliani:
Sleeping Nude, Arms Opened (1917).

Jules Pascin (right), Pierre Marseille and two young models (photo).

Jules Pascin: **Young Girl in Rose** (1912).

Jules Pascin: **Rest.**

257

Photograph of Jeanne Hébuterne.

Amedeo Modigliani:
Portrait of Jeanne Hébuterne.

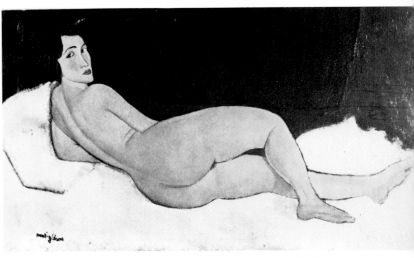

Amedeo Modigliani: **Nude Lying on Left Side** (1917).

Jeanne Hébuterne: **Self Portrait** (1916).

Henri Rousseau: **The Dream** (1910).

Kees Van Dongen: **Tranquility** (1918).

E very painter had his own vision of Woman. She might have been a model or friend, like the dauntless and talented Jeanne Hébuterne, who lived and worked with Modigliani. For Douanier Rousseau, she was Yadwigha, a young Polish woman for whom he had an unrequited passion and whom he posed in a manner similar to that of Manet's **Olympia.** For Van Dongen, Woman appears as a fantasy, as in his double head to foot nude, both enigmatic and ambiguous.

The artists all sought the Eternal Woman—whether as mother, sister, daughter, mistress or wife.

260

Henri Matisse: **The Dance** (1910).

"**I** had to decorate a three-story home. I imagined a visitor entering there. He had to make an effort to climb the stairs, and he had a real need to be reinvigorated. That's why the first panel represented a dance at the summit of a hill." This was Matisse's explanation of the idea behind his *Dance*. Matisse felt that "We will reach a higher serenity through the simplification of ideas and plastic means." The decorative concerns of Kisling's **Nude on a Red Divan** do not hold back his expressionist needs. The melancholy of the reclining woman belongs only to the artist.

More than any other subject, the nude enables the painter to externalize his desires and to understand and conquer his inhibitions.

Moïse Kisling: **Nude on a Red Divan** (1918).

Moïse Kisling: **Jean Cocteau** (1916).

Amedeo Modigliani: **Self Portrait.**

Two scandals that erupted in 1917 caused quite a rumpus in the cafés and salons frequented by the art world. The first was Modigliani's exhibition of his Nudes, and the second was the creation of the ballet **Parade.**

Modigliani's emaciated features are revealed in his **Self Portrait,** yet he was overjoyed at the opportunity to put his motto: "Your only duty is to save your dream," into practice. Yet despite the encouragement of his friends and the poet Blaise Cendrar's preface to the exhibition catalogue in which he evoked the "ebb and flow of passion" in Modigliani's interior world, the public was more outraged than impressed. The police were alerted; art was arrested where the illusion began.

Jean Cocteau, (who dreamed of "hearing the music of Picasso's guitars") plotted with Diaghelev to persuade Picasso to design and paint the curtains, décor and costumes for Erik Satie's 'Realist Ballet' **Parade.** Cocteau had some difficulty, but Picasso eventually agreed to undertake the project. The public entered the theater intrigued by the "burlesque scene" at the doors, but left in indignation. A disgruntled spectator grumbled: "If I had known it was going to be so silly, I'd have brought my children." There was no less scandal created within the ranks of the rear guard Cubists who were unhappy about Picasso's participation in what they considered a frivolous project. As Cocteau explained, "A dictatorship rules over Montmartre and Montparnasse. One is crossing into the austere period of Cubism. The objects on a café table and a Spanish guitar are the only pleasures allowed. To paint a décor, especially for the Ballet Russe, was a crime. Picasso's acceptance of my proposition horrified the denizens of the Rotunde Café." Following his own independent nature, and in love with Olga, one of the dancers from the Ballet Russe, Picasso headed toward a new art that would be Ingresgue and Classical.

Tullio Garbari: **Intellectuals at the Rotonde** (1916).

Pablo Picasso: **The Curtain for Parade** (1917).

Kisling, Pâquerette and Picasso at Montparnasse (photo).

Left to right:
Ortiz de Zarate, Kisling,
Max Jacob, Picasso
and Pâquerette (photo).

Pablo Picasso: **Portrait of Erik Satie.**

263

Robert Delaunay: **Windows Opening Simultaneously** (1912).

Marcel Duchamp: **Nude Descending Staircase** (1912).

Fernand Léger: **Card Game** (1917).

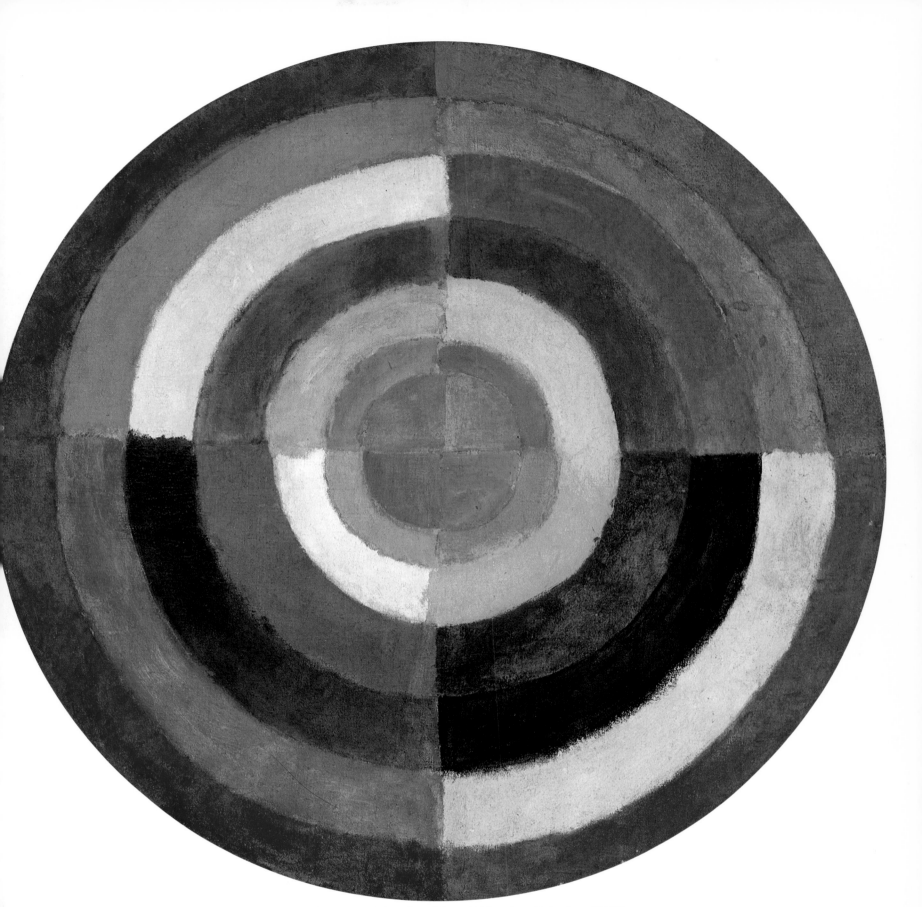

Robert Delaunay: **Disk, First Non-Objective Painting** (1912).

"You will raise the curtain
And now the window is opened…
Oh Paris
From red to green all yellow dies
The window opens itself like an orange
The beautiful fruit of light."
In his free verse on Robert Delaunay's **Windows,**
Guillaume Apollinaire persuaded the painters to take
life into consideration and the world to heart.

Marcel Duchamp had already enabled art to descend
from its pedestal and, through its internal vitality,
"escape from the prison of tradition."

The workers' herald, Fernand Léger, stated that "our
need for joy, emulation and action is reinforced by
color." Léger discovered on the battlefields that war
condemns man to fraternity: one must struggle to
preserve the cards of one's destiny. From their
window, Robert and Sonia Delaunay watched the stars
and made colors detonate and scatter with cosmic gaiety,
fulfilling our universal thirst for pure beauty.

265

Following in the painters' footsteps

Barbizon and Chailly-en-Bière in Fontainebleau Forest

Courtyard of the White Horse Inn. In the background, the steeple of the church at Chailly-en-Bière.

The best way to discover or rediscover Barbizon is through the forest of Fontainebleau. Do as the pilgrim-painters did and cover it on foot. When you reach Barbizon imagine that you'll be greeted, as the painters were, by *père* Ganne, his wife and their dog, Ronflot. Visit the Ganne Inn, which is now a charming museum containing the wooden panels and furniture painted by the Barbizon artists.

Along the Grande Rue and its side-streets you'll find numerous comfortable hostels and inns. All of these inns can provide you with maps for forest walks that will take you through the clusters of oaks, beeches and pines. The fresh earthy scent of the mushrooms and wild herbs en route to the Apremont Gorge is intoxicating.

Should you linger late in the day on these footpaths surrounded by trembling ferns, you too will believe in the romantic pantheism that moved the pre-Impressionists. You'll hear the breathing and sighing of the forest, the buzzing of insects, the unexpected cries of birds, the snorting of boar and the hoofbeats of stags in the clearings. These sounds fill the forest today as they did thousands of years ago. Follow them, lose yourself, pursue your own pilgrimage to the sources of the Barbizon school's inspiration and meditation. Try to see your surroundings through the eyes of Corot, Rousseau, Barye, Diaz, Ziem and Millet, whose reinventions of landscapes led the way for the Impressionists. You'll understand their desire to render homage to nature.

If you go to Bas Bréau you'll find the bronze plaques honoring Millet and Rousseau. Their profiles are united in the rocks as they are united in their twin tombs at the cemetery at Chailly-en-

Entrance to the Millet Museum.

Entrance to the Théodore Rousseau Museum.

Bière. Go there and listen to the blue tits and nightingales singing above the mossy graves.

Enter Barbizon by the *Portes aux Vaches* ("Cow Gates"). You'll pass by groups of tourists who've come from all over the world to see the bell tower that appears in Millet's *Angelus*.

If you climb the Grande Rue at Barbizon you'll want to stop in front of the farm houses once inhabited by the artists. Although closed to the public, these houses bear commemorative plaques telling who lived there and when.

You can visit Millet's former studio which is now a museum containing his furniture and painting equipment, and even a hint of the man himself. The studio of Théodore Rousseau is a municipal museum which is rich in documentation. Both buildings are covered with lovely weeping wisteria.

Along with the Ganne Inn, the *Cheval Blanc* (The White Horse Inn) at Chailly-en-Bière merits a visit. Few art lovers realize that this former post stop has hardly changed since its early days. It is wonderful to see its modest dining room filled with the paintings that bore witness to its excellent cooking.

Heads of Millet and Rousseau sculpted in the rocks at Bas Bréau.

269

Honfleur
and the Normandy
Coast

The Old Dock at Honfleur.

André Malraux Museum at Le Havre.

Honfleur, on the Normandy coast, will tempt you as it tempted the privileged artists who flocked there. Visit the *Vieux Bassin* (The Old Dock) and marvel at the reflection of the yachts in the water. It was here that Rabelais' gigantic hero, Pantagruel, embarked for the Kingdom of Utopia. Lean against the now peaceful cannons that serve as moorings and think of the schooners that once set off for Quebec, Martinique or Louisiana.

Follow the movement of the clouds over the Seine's currents and watch them change forms and cast shadows over the water. You'll understand the fascination that they held for the Saint-Siméon artists.

Honfleur—port of poets, painters and humorists, where the unusual melodies of Erik Satie seem to fill the night air. Viewed from above, at night, it seems as if the city is lit by hundreds of candles extending as far as the lonely lighthouse.

Wander through the streets near the Old Dock and pay a visit to Sainte-Catherine's whose pointing tower caught the eye of Jongkind and Boudin.

Visit the chapel of Notre-Dame-de-Grâce with its model sail boats and from the heights watch the sunset over the Seine's estuary. An equally panoramic

The beach and cliffs at Etretat.

The restaurant at the Saint-Siméon farm.

view can be had from the cliffs at Étretat, whose majesty fascinated Monet all his life.

The beaches at Deauville and Sainte-Adresse are no longer populated with Boudin's veiled women carrying colorful parasols or Dufy's gentlemen wearing straw boaters. However, you will be able to find these men and women in the paintings at the museums in Honfleur, Le Havre and Trouville. At the Boudin Museum, the large bay windows offer you the chance to admire the views that were transposed to the canvases of these masters.

Above all, do not forget to visit the Saint-Siméon farm. The Toutain's successors will offer you delectable fish and unforgettable wines for a superb finishing touch to your visit.

The beach at Sainte-Adresse.

On the banks of the Seine and its tributaries

Before you set off to explore the river Seine and the actual sites of so many Impressionist paintings, a visit to the Musée d'Orsay-Jeu de Paume is an absolute must.

Having filled your head with those wonderful images, do as Daubigny and Monet did and explore the Seine by boat or barge. Leave from the Pont des Arts in Paris and follow the Seine to Honfleur and the port at Le Havre—you'll then understand how Impressionism was born along this route.

Near Chatou you'll find the *Maison Fournaise,* the site of Renoir's *Boatmens Lunch,* preserved in its original state. Picnic on the riverbanks and, if you're there in June, you'll be able to participate in the costumed festivities and colorful regattas that celebrate the *Belle Epoch.*

At Argenteuil you'll see the magic of the nautical village that attracted Monet, Renoir, Manet, Sisley and Caillebotte.

Asnières, less glamorous than Argenteuil, is just as important in the development of Seurat's Neo-Impressionism. Don't forget Port-Marly, Marly-le-Roi and its Queens Park; Louveciennes and Saint-Germain-en-Laye, where Maurice Denis and his Nabis friends await you at his former home at Prieuré. At Conflans-Sainte-Honorine you'll find the water transport museum that fascinated the artists who painted barges and river traffic. At Pontoise there is a museum dedicated to Pissarro, who spent most of his life there. At Auvers-sur-Oise you'll find the 13th century church painted by Van Gogh; Daubigny's studio; and the Ravoux Inn, Van Gogh's last home. Also at Auvers are the graves of Vincent and

The church at Auvers-sur-Oise.

Park in Marly-le-Roi.

272

River barge.

Lily pond at Giverny.

The Fournaise home at Chatou.

his brother Théo, along with a statue of Vincent by the sculptor Zadkine. The charming village of Vétheuil, captured on the canvases of Monet, is also worth a visit. In fact, an entire guidebook could be filled with recommendations of places to visit in this area.

Don't forget the city of Rouen, whose cathedral has been immortalized by Monet, Turner, Pissarro and many other painters. Rouen also contains a very rich Museum of Fine Arts, which is a must.

Finally, follow Monet to his favorite masterpiece—Giverny. Spend the day in his gardens, picnic beside the lily ponds and visit his home with its blue and yellow rooms filled with a superb collection of Japanese prints. At Giverny you'll see Monet's canvases come to life before your eyes.

The Ravoux Inn at Auvers-sur-Oise.

Pont-Aven and Le Pouldu on the Brittany coast

L'Argoat, meaning "land of wood," is the Celtic name for the interior of Brittany, and l'Armor, Celtic for "on the sea," are both full of multicolored and multiformed charm. Surrender yourself to their beauty and let them take possession of you in the same way that the fairies were said to have kidnapped the Breton youths of old.

Begin by following the creeks that seek to rejoin the rocky coastal areas swallowed by the sea. Explore the water mills at Pont-Aven and follow the rivers. Cross the fields where the skulls of giants are crowned in thick golden gorse. You'll find thatched cottages surrounded by rickety fences overlooking corn fields. Enter the chapels where you will be greeted by the innocent smiles of the sculptured saints.

"On that granite earth marched a primitive race as fine as the sands," said Michelet. Walk in his footsteps. Enjoy the local festivities and *Pardons* (Breton religious celebrations), marriages and

One of the mills at Pont-Aven.

The *Café de la Plage* at Pouldu, formerly Marie Poupée's Inn.

The former Gloanec Pension at Pont-Aven.

Notre-Dame de la Paix chapel in Pouldu.

Saint-Maudet chapel in Pouldu.

masses that are recreated today by the region's folklorists. If you are in the area on the first Sunday in August don't miss the Flower Festival at Pont-Aven.

After following the route of the Aven river as far as the Gargantua Rocks, stop at the Rosmadec Mill for a meal and then make your way to the large square where you'll find the Julia sisters' Hotel. The Julia sisters were the first to transform that village of carpenters ("Pont-Aven, city of renown... 14 water mills, 15 houses") into the city of painters, whose works can be seen at the municipal museum.

Cross the bridge at Pont-Aven and you'll rediscover the Gloanec Pension in the square where the market is held. The Pension has been transformed into the *Maison de la Presse* where you'll find postcards and a commemorative plaque recalling its once celebrated guests.

Venture into the *Bois d'Amour* (Wood of Love)—its innumerable sighs and whispers will communicate the magnetism that it held for the young maids and artists who roamed these woods. Visit the Tremalo chapel where you'll find the crucifix that inspired Gauguin's *Yellow Christ*.

Like Gauguin and his young friends, move on to Pouldu via the Clohars-Carnoet forest. When you arrive at Pouldu go down to the Great Sands Beach where you'll see the neighboring inn that was once owned by Marie Poupé (now the Café de la Plage). Visit the lovely chapel of the Notre-Dame-de-la-Paix as well as that of Saint-Maudet, at the heights of Pouldu. You'll be reminded of Filiger and the young Bretons who became saints on his canvases. Finally, visit the charming beach at Bellangenêt, where the rector, seeing a boy posing nude for Filiger, believed that he was tempted by the devil.

Batignolles, Montmartre and Montparnasse

Place du Tertre and *Sacré-Cœur* at Montmartre.

Max Jacob liked to repeat Heraclitus' adage that "One never swims twice in the same river." And Guillaume Apollinaire, looking at his image reflected in the river from the Mirabeau bridge, found inspiration for two of his loveliest lines: "joy always comes after sorrow," and, "the days pass but I remain." You too will have these lines in mind when you cross and recross the Seine in the path of the painters who, crossed it on foot or in buses, navigated from one river bank to the other, from Batignolles and Montmartre to Montparnasse.

What's become of their friends? Where have all their emotions, sorrows and joys gone? What have they done with the houses and studios, streets and squares, bistros and cabarets, which formed the gilded frames of their Bohemian lives? The answers can be found in the canvases that you'll see at the Museum of Modern Art for the City of Paris, the Tokyo Palace, the Orangerie, the National

The *Moulin de la Galette*.

The *Moulin Rouge*.

Museum of Modern Art at the Pompidou Center, the Orsay Museum-Jeu de Paume, the Marmottan Museum and the Montmartre Museum.

It's best to have visited these museums and seen the paintings before exploring the sections of Paris where they were created. Even if some of the actual buildings have been demolished, changed or moved, you'll have an idea of how they once appeared.

The *Ruche* ("The Beehive") still exists at 52 rue Dantzig in the 15th Arrondissement. Unfortunately, the *Bateau Lavoir* ("The Wash House") was burned in a fire in 1970 and has since been rebuilt at No. 13 place Émile-Goudreau. This little square with its Wallace fountain is worth a visit.

At the Montmartre Museum there are complete models of the former studios of *Bateau Lavoir*. The museum is just beyond the vineyards, in the former country house of Molière's friend Claude de Rosimond.

Sacré-Cœur (Basilica of the Sacred Heart), located at the top of the Butte of Montmartre, offers a spectacular view of Paris. Nearby is the Place du Tertre, filled with street artists and cafés, which give it its village atmosphere. At No. 21 place du Tertre is the house of the Free Commune, founded in the 1920's to keep the traditions of the Old Butte alive.

Place Clichy.

Le Dôme on Boulevard Montparnasse.

La Ruche, 52 rue Dantzig.

Take a walk along rue Cortot and pay a visit to No. 12, which housed many artists, including Renoir, Dufy, Suzanne Valadon and her son Utrillo. Here Renoir improvised a studio in order to work on his *Moulin de la Galette.* The gardens behind the house were the setting for his other celebrated canvas *The Swing.* This country house is a living museum, filled with souvenirs of the artists who lived there. Its gardens descend to the rue Saint-Vincent and rejoin the *Lapin Agile* (Agile Rabbit) where traditional literary evenings still take place today.

Passing along the rue Lepic you'll see the restored *Moulin de la Galette.* Continue down toward the "Lower Montmartre" where you'll find Place Pigalle, the Place Blanche and the *Moulin Rouge,* all leading to the Place Clichy—an important crossroads between Montmartre and Batignolles. Take a detour via rue Hégésippe-Moreau where you'll find the former studios of Cézanne, Signac, Marcoussis and Eugène Carrière at No. 15. It was here that the art dealer Ambroise Vollard posed 114 times for Cézanne.

The Vavins crossroads at Montparnasse, with its *Dome* and *Rotonde* brasseries standing sentinel on each side of the Boulevard Montparnasse, is where the young painters and poets migrated beginning in 1910. The School of Paris filled its ranks from the habitués of these two brasseries. Drink a toast to the

Vineyards below the Montmartre Museum.

memory of the painters, poets and intellectuals and to their sense of daring and innovation.

Stroll along the Boulevard Raspail, where there are still many artists' studios in the side streets and *cul-de-sacs* (Impasse du Maine, rue Vercingétorix) inhabited by a considerable number of artist with world-wide reputations.

At the *Coupole* on the Boulevard Montparnasse you'll find some of the cosmopolitan ambience of Montparnasse nigh life. However it is really at the *Closerie des Lilas,* where the poet Paul Fort and his friends gathered in 1913, that you'll be able to sense the atmosphere of those days. The attraction of the *Closerie des Lilas* is reinforced by its proximity to the Luxembourg Gardens. Take a stroll along the tree-lined paths running beside the pool shaded by plane trees. In the center of the gardens you'll find children navigating sail boats under the fountain just as they did a century ago. Near the Orangerie, on the side of the park bordering Saint-Sulpice, there is a splendid monument by Dalou which is dedicated to Delacroix and the glory of art.

Explore Paris with the paintings, poems and songs of these artists in mind and you too will share in their joy and understand the sources behind their creations.

Luxembourg Gardens.

La Closerie des Lilas at the Obervatoire crossroads.

La Rotonde at Vavin crossroads.

279

Sources of Illustrations

Unless otherwise indicated, all the paintings listed here are painted in oil on canvas. I have assigned identification numbers to the works, going in this order: top, left to right; bottom, left to right. The dimensions are given in meters: height by width. The location of the signature is indicated as follows: S: signed; D: Dated; b.r.: bottom right; b.l.: bottom left; t.r.: top right; t.l.: top left.

4 Claude Monet: *Study for Luncheon on the Grass.* Detail (see p. 54). Ph. Snark.

6 Claude Monet: *Camille Monet and her Cousin on the Beach at Trouville.* Detail (see p. 79).

8 Édouard Manet: *Café-Concert,* 1879 (0.999 × 0.780). S.D.b.l. National Gallery, London.

10 Honoré Daumier: *The Politics of Beer Drinkers.* Coll. Dr. O. Renhart. Ph. Arch. Ed. du Temps.

13 Pablo Picasso: *Composition of Bread and Fruit on a Table,* 1909 (1.640 × 1.325). Kunstmuseum, Basel. Ph. Hinz-Ziolo. © Spadem 1983.

20 Gustave Courbet: *Bonjour Monsieur Courbet,* 1854. Detail.

21 Gustave Courbet: *Bonjour Monsieur Courbet,* 1854. D.S.b.r. (1.29 × 1.49). Musée Fabre, Montpellier. Ph. Réunion des Musées Nat.

26 1. Arch. E.R.L.
2. Camille Corot: *Fontainebleau, road to Orléans* (0.258 × 0.402). S.b.l. Graphite on paper. Louvre, Paris. Cabinet des Dessins. Ph. Réunion des Musées Nat.
3. Caruelle d'Aligny: *View of Quarries at Fontainebleau forest.* (1.63 × 2.15). S.b.l. Musée Bargoin, Clermont-Ferrand. Photo. Library C.R.D.P.
4. Auguste Anastasi: *Fontainebleau Forest, Wolves Gorge,* 1858. J.-F. Millet Home and Studio, Barbizon. Ph. E.R.L.

27 1. Camille Corot: *Rocks in Fontainebleau Forest* (0.459 × 0.585). S.b.r. National Gallery of Art, Washington D.C. (Chester Dale Coll.).
2. Ph. Porcheron (J. Sagne Collection).

28 1. Ph. Anonymous D.R.
2. Attributed to Honoré Daumier: *Portrait of Théodore Rousseau.* (0.31 × 0.21). In lower corner "To my friend Théodore Rousseau, Daumier." Ph. Giraudon.
3. Théodore Rousseau: *The Oak,* 1861 (0.124 × 0.157). S.D.b.r. Etching. Coll. Mme Jacque.

29 1. Narcisse Diaz de la Peña: *Rocks at Fontainebleau,* c. 1840-45. (0.22 × 0.35). Oil on wood. Musée de la ville de Fontainebleau. Ph. M. Decruck.
2. Camille Corot: *Corot at his easel,* c. 1825. Paper mounted on canvas. (0.325 × 0.245). Louvre, Paris. Ph. Réunion des Musées Nat.
3. Alexandre Véron: *Millet, Rousseau and Véron at Wolves Gorge.* S.b.r. Charcoal. Coll. Mme I. Fasono. Ph. E.R.L.

30 1. *The Ascension of Painters in the Forest.* Panel decorating Ganne Inn. Oil on wood. Attrib. Alexis Mossa. Musée de l'Auberge Ganne, Barbizon. Ph. Miltos Toscas.
2. *The Barbizon Coach.* Private Collection. Ph. E.R.L.
3. Olivier de Penne: *Barbizon Festivities,* Drawing on wood for *Illustration* 5/29/1858. Ph. E.R.L.
4-5. Xavier de Cock: *Portraits of Mr. and Mrs. Ganne,* 1854. Pencil (0.135 × 0.180). Private Coll. Ph. E.R.L.
6. Ph. G. Demais. E.R.L.

31 1. *Good Painters Chasing Bad Painters From the Ganne Inn.* Panel decoration Ganne Inn. Oil on wood. Attrib. Alexis Mossa. Musée de l'Auberge Ganne, Bar-

bizon. Ph. Miltos Tosca.
2. Charles Jacque: *Entrance to Ganne Inn.* Engraving. Musée de l'Auberge Ganne, Barbizon. Ph. E.R.L.
3. *Courtyard of Ganne Inn.* Engraving. Musée de l'Auberge Ganne, Barbizon. Ph. E.R.L.
4-5. Pannels at Ganne Inn. Musée de l'Auberge Ganne. Ph. Miltos Toscas.

32 1. Anonymous portrait of *père Ganne.* Graphite (0.47 × 0.39). Musée de l'Auberge Ganne, Barbizon. Ph. E.R.L.
2. Anonymous portrait of Mrs. Ganne. Charcoal (0.75 × 0.62). Musée de l'Auberge Ganne. Ph. E.R.L.
3. Guest register Ganne Inn, 1848. Gauthier Coll. Ph. E.R.L.
4. Olivier de Penne: *Wedding Dinner.* Oil on wood (0.93 × 1.05). Musée de l'Auberge Ganne, Barbizon. Ph. G. Demais. E.R.L.
5. Guest register Ganne Inn. Musée de l'Auberge Ganne. Barbizon. Ph. E.R.L.

33 1. Buffet door, Ganne Inn. Detail. Oil on wood. Private coll. Ph. G. Demais E.R.L.
2. Wardrobe door Ganne Inn. Oil on wood. Private Coll. Ph. G. Demais E.R.L.
3. Cupboard door Ganne Inn. Oil on wood. Musée de l'Auberge Ganne, Barbizon. Ph. Miltos Toscas.
4. *Painters Bacchanalia.* Composition on barn door Ganne Inn. Ph. G. Demais E.R.L.
5. Buffet at Ganne Inn. Musée de l'Auberge Ganne, Barbizon. Ph. Miltos Toscas.

34 1. Camille Corot: *Stamati Bulgari Painting,* c. 1835. Graphite on grey paper. (0.139 × 0.19). Louvre, Paris. Cbt. des Dessins. Ph. Réunion des Musées Nat.
2. Charles Jacque: *The Stable.* Coll. Mme Jacque. Ph. G. Demais E.R.L.
3. Charles Sauvageot: *Artists Inn at Barbizon.* Engraving for *Illustration* 03/13/1875. Ph. Bib. Nat. Paris.
4. Camille Corot: Handwritten notes on painting. Ph. Bibl. Nat. Paris.

35 1. Camille Corot: *Fontainebleau, Farm Courtyard,* c. 1860-65 (0.49 × 0.56). S.b.l. Private coll.
2. Camille Corot, July 1873. Ph. Desavary. St. Nicholas-les-Arras.
3. Camille Corot: *Young Boy in High Hat,* 1822-23 (0.21 × 0.22). S.b.l. Private Coll. Paris. Ph. Réunion des Musées Nat.

36 1. Ph. G. Demais. E.R.L.
2. Ph. Esparcieux. Arch. E.R.L.
3. Georges Gassies: *Théodore Rousseau's House.* S.b.r. Musée Théodore Rousseau, Barbizon. Ph. G. Demais. E.R.L.
4. Théodore Rousseau. Photo.
5. Georges Gassies: *Self Portrait.* Private Coll., Barbizon. Ph. G. Demais. E.R.L.

37 1. Théodore Rousseau: *The Forest in Winter,* begun in 1846 (1.62 × 2.60). Metropolitan Museum, N.Y.C.
2. Arch. E.R.L.
3. Théodore Rousseau: *Entrance to Forest,* Drawing. S.b.r. Mme Jacque; Musée Théodore Rousseau, Barbizon.

38 1. Théodore Rousseau: *Painter at Work in the Forest.* Drawing. Stamp b.r. Musée Théodore Rousseau, Barbizon.

2. Louis-Philippe Crossroads, Fontainebleau Forest. Ph. Arch. E.R.L.
3. Théodore Rousseau: *Sunset, Fontainebleau Forest,* 1849-50 (1.420 × 1.975). S.b.l. Louvre, Paris. Ph. Réunion des Musées Nat.
4. Théodore Rousseau: Illustrated signature. 1865. Musée Théodore Rousseau, Barbizon. Ph. E.R.L.

39 1. Théodore Rousseau: *Fontainebleau Forest After a Storm,* c. 1860-65 (0.30 × 0.51). S.b.r. Louvre, Paris. Ph. Réunion des Musées Nat.
2. Théodore Rousseau: *The Cart,* 1862. Oil on wood. (0.28 × 0.53). S.b.r. Louvre, Paris. Ph. Réunion des Musées Nat.

40 1. Jean-François Millet: *Self Portrait,* 1845-46 Blurred charcoal drawing and black paper on grey-blue paper. (0.562 × 0.456). Louvre, Paris Cbt. des Dessins. Ph. E.R.L.
2. Copy of Drawing by J.-F. Millet: *Portrait of Catherine Lemaire.* 1848-49. Draawing in black pencil with white highlights on grey-blue paper. Coll. Georges Petit. Maison et Atelier J.-F. Millet. Ph. E.R.L.
3. Ph. Arch. E.R.L.
4. Georges Cassies: *Millet's Studio,* 1863. S.b.r.-D.b.l. Maison et Atelier J.-F. Millet, Barbizon. Ph. E.R.L.
5. Bibl. Nat. Paris. Arch. E.R.L.

41 1. J.-F. Millet's house at Barbizon in 1875. Arch. E.R.L.
2. Jean-François Millet: *Millet's Garden at Barbizon.* Black pencil drawing (0.297 × 0.372). Musée Bonnat, Bayonne. Ph. C.N.M.H.S. © Spadem 1983.
3. Jean-François Millet: *Millet's House at Barbizon.* S.b.r. NY Carlsberg Clyptotek, Copenhagen. Arch. Ed. du Temps.
4. J.-F. Millet's palette. Maison et Atelier J.-F. Millet, Barbizon. Ph. G. Demais. E.R.L.

42 1. Barbizon painters with Millet, Courbet and Grigoresco. Coll. Pr. G. Opresco, Director Historical Institute of the Roumanian Academy of Art.
2. Gustave Courbet: *Stonebreaker.* Bibl. Nat. Paris.
3. Jean-François Millet. Ph. Cuvelier, 1862.
4. Gustave Courbet: *Corn Winnowers.* 1854 (1.31 × 1.67). S.D.b.l. Musée des Beaux Arts, Nantes. Ph. Giraudon.
5. Jean-François Millet: *Shepherd Showing the Way to Travellers,* 1857. Drawing in pencil and pastel. (0.355 × 0.495). Corcoran Gallery of Art, Washington D.C.

43 1. Gustave Courbet: *Stonebreaker,* 1849. Detail. Destroyed during W.W.II. Ph. Bulloz.
2. Jean-François Millet: *Study for Winnower* Lead pencil drawing. (0.243 × 0.232). Bibl. Nat. Paris.
3. Jean-François Millet: *Noon* second panel of *Four Hours of the Day.* Bibl. Nat. Paris.
4. Jean-François Millet: *The Winnower,* replica of 1848 painting. Oil on wood. (0.795 × 0.585). Louvre, Paris. Ph. Réunion des Musées Nat.
5. Vincent Van Gogh: *The Siesta,* after

Millet. 1889 (0.73 × 0.91). Musée Orsay-Jeu de Paume. Ph. Réunion des Musées Nat.

44-45 Jean-François Millet: *The Angelus,* 1858-59 (0.555 × 0.660). S.b.r. Louvre, Paris. Ph. Réunion des Musées Nat.
1. Jean-François Millet: *The Angelus,* 1858-59 (0.555 × 0.660). S.b.r. Louvre, Paris. Ph. Réunion des Musées Nat.

46 2. Ph. G. Demais. E.R.L.
3. Jean-François Millet: *The Siesta,* 1858. Detail. Lead pencil and pastel drawing. (0.362 × 0.462). S.b.r. Musée des Beaux Arts, Reims. Ph. Bulloz.
4. *The Angelus.* Novel by R. Esse. Maison et Atelier J.-F. Millet. Ph. G. Demias. E.R.L.
5. Mrs. Moshler called the "Belle Marie" who posed for *The Angelus.* Maison et Atelier Jean-François Millet. Ph. Esparcieux.

47 1. Jean-François Millet: *Leaving for Work,* 1863. Etching (0.385 × 0.310). Bibl. Nat. Paris Arch. E.R.L.
2. Ph. G. Demais. E.R.L.
3. Félix Ziem: *Chailly Plains,* c. 1860-65. Watercolor (0.140 × 0.245). S.b.r. Musée de Petit-Palais, Paris. Ph. Bulloz.
4. Jean-François Millet: *Church at Chailly.* Pastel (0.69 × 0.85). Ph. Galerie Durand-Ruel. Arch. Éd. du Temps.

48 1. Jean-François Millet: *The Gleaners,* 1857 (0.835 × 1.100). Louvre, Paris. Ph. Réunion des Musées Nat.
2. Jean-François Millet: *The Gleaners.* Study in conté crayon (0.295 × 0.440). Stamp b.r. Musée Grobet-Labadié, Marseille.
3. Autochrome. Personnal Collection. S.F.P.

49 1. Jean-François Millet: *Twilight.* Pencil and pastel on yellow paper (0.508 × 0.387). S.b.r. Museum of Fine Arts, Boston. Quincy Adams Gift.
2. Jean-François Millet: *Shepherd Watching his Flock,* 1872-74. Black and brown pencil drawing. (0.295 × 0.380). Musée des Beaux-Arts, Reims. Ph. Bulloz.
3. Sheep on Chailly-en-Bière plain. Ph. Arch. E.R.L.

50 1. Ph. G. Demais. E.R.L.
2. Ph. Siron. Arch. E.R.L.
3. Portraits of Proprietors of White Horse Inn. Mural painting. Ph. G. Demais. E.R.L.
4. Mural sketches. White Horse Inn. Ph. Miltos Toscas.
5. Ph. Miltos Toscas.
6. Ph. G. Demais. E.R.L.
1. Charles Moreau-Vauthier: *Portrait of Young Woman.* Mural painting. S.D.b.r. Ph. G. Demais. E.R.L.
2-3. Mural sketches at White Horse Inn. Ph. G. Demais. E.R.L.
4. Frédéric Bazille: *Monet after His Accident,* 1865 (0.47 × 0.65). Musée du Jeu de Paume, Paris. Ph. Réunion des Musées Nat.

52 1. Rosa Bonheur: *Study of Stags.* Musée de la ville de Fontainebleau. Ph. Réunion des Musées Nat.
2. Rosa Bonheur in her studio. Musée des Beaux-Arts, Bordeaux. Arch. E.R.L.
3. Antoine-Louis Bayre: *Two Panthers on the Dunes at Fontainebleau.* Watercolor.

Louvre, Paris. Cbt. des Dessins. Ph. Réunion des Musées Nat.
4. Ph. Collection Sirot-Angel.
5. Gustave Courbet: *The Hunted Stag,* 1867 (1.11 × 0.85). S.D.b.l. Louvre, Paris Ph. Réunion des Musées Nat.

53 1. Alfred Sisley: *Village Street in Marlotte,* 1866 (0.65 × 0.92). S.D.b.r. Albright-Knox Art Gallery, Buffalo, N.Y. General Purchase Funds, 1956.
2. Auguste Renoir: *At the Inn of Mother Anthony,* 1866 (1.95 × 1.30). National Museum, Stockholm. © Spadem 1983.

54 1. Claude Monet: *Study for Luncheon on the Grass,* 1866 (1.320 × 1.855). Pushkin Museum, Moscow. © Spadem 1983.
2. Paul Cézanne: *Fontainebleau, effect of snow,* 1879-80 (0.735 1.07). S.b.l. Museum of Modern Art, New York. Gift of André Meyer.
3. Gustave Courbet: *Hunt Meal.* Wallraf Richard Museum. Kôln.
4. Photo. c. 1865. Arch. E.R.L.

55 1. Claude Monet: *The Chailly Route,* c. 1865 (0.43 × 0.59). S.b.l. Musée du Jeu de Paume, Paris. Ph. Réunion des Musées Nat. © Spadem 1983.
2. Ph. Arch. E.R.L.
3. Ph. Arch. E.R.L.

56 1. Eugène Boudin: *White Clouds, Blue Sky.* Sky study c. 1859. Pastel on paper (0.15 × 1.20). S.b.r. Musée Eugène Boudin, Honfleur. Eugène Boudin legacy 1899. Ph. G. Demais. E.R.L.

57 1. Michel Lévy: E. Boudin painting animals in a meadow near Deauville, 1880 (0.22 × 0.27). Musée Eugène Boudin, Honfleur. Ph. G. Demais. E.R.L.

62 1. Louis-Alexandre Dubourg: *Normandy* (Drawing from unpublished notebook). Graphite and conté crayon. Musée Eugène-Boudin, Honfleur. Don. Mme Schlumberger.
2. *Norman Woman,* c. 1859. Portrait thought to be of Mother Toutain. Oil on wooden panel (0.21 × 0.27). Musée Eugène-Boudin, Honfleur Eugène Boudin legacy. Ph. G. Demais. E.R.L.
3. Arch. E.R.L.
4. Louis-Alexandre Dubourg: *Cat* (Drawing from unpublished notebook). Graphite and conté crayon. Musée Eugène-Boudin, Honfleur. Don. Mme Schlumberger.

63 1. Camille Corot: *The Toutain Farm.* Bridgestone Museum of Art, Tokyo.
2. Adolphe-Félix Cals: *Honfleur Women Unravelling Yarn,* 1877 (0.35 × 0.27). Roland Boelen Coll. Honfleur.
3. Claude Monet: *Farmyard in Normandy* (c. 1863). S.b.r. (0.65 × 0.80). Musée du Jeu de Paume, Paris. Ph. Réunion des Musées Nat. © Spadem 1983.

64 1. Louis-Alexandre Dubourg: *Tables at Saint-Siméon.* S.b.r. Musée de Trouville.
2. Louis-Alexandre Dubourg: *Lunch at Saint-Siméon Farm.* Drawing (0.15 × 0.21). Musée Eugène-Boudin, Honfleur. Legs. Désiré Louveau, 1937.
3. Louis-Alexandre Dubourg: *Dog and her puppies* (drawing from unpublished sketchbook). Graphite and conté crayon. Musée Eugène-Boudin, Honfleur. Don Mme Schlumberger.

65 1. Eugène Boudin: *Drinkers at Saint-Siméon Farm* (c. 1859). Oil on wooden panel (0.13 × 0.23). S.b.r. Musée Eugène-Boudin, Honfleur. Legs Désiré Louveau, 1937.
2-3. André Gill: *Sign for the Saint-Siméon Farm* and engraving of the same. Roland Boelen Coll. Honfleur.
4. Eugène Boudin: *At the Saint-Siméon Farm with Jongkind, E. Van Marcke, C. Monet, père Achard.* Watercolor (0.14 × 0.18). Private coll. D.R.

66 1. Ph. Arch. E.R.L.
2. Paul Huet: *Apple Trees on the Grace Coast,* 1829. Oil on wooden panel (0.235 × 0.310). Gift of Mme Katia Granoff. Ph. Schuller.
3. Adolphe-Félix Cals: *Lunch at Honfleur,* 1875. S.D.b.l. Musée d'Orsay, Paris. Ph. Giraudon.

67 1. Autochrome. Coll. S.F.P. Fotogram.
2. Ph. Arch. E.R.L.
3. Eugène Boudin: *Still Life with Leg of Lamb,* c. 1859 (0.215 × 0.35). Musée Eugène-Boudin. Legs. Eugène Boudin 1899. Ph. G. Demais. E.R.L.
4. Eugène Boudin: *The Saint-Siméon Farm.* Pastel c. 1859 (0.135 × 0.200). Musée Eugène-Boudin, Honfleur. Legs Eugène Boudin. Ph. G. Demais. E.R.L.

68 1. Ph. P. Poullain. N.P.I.
2. Johan Barthold Jongkind: *Grace Chapel, Honfleur,* 14 September 1864. S.D. (0.36 × 0.48). Coll. Mr. & Mrs. E.V. Thaw, New York.
3. Claude Monet: *Chapel of Notre-Dame de Grace,* 1864 (0.52 × 0.68). Private Coll. D.R. © Spadem 1983.
4. Louis-Alexandre Dubourg: *Chapel of Notre-Dame-de-Grace,* 1867. Drawing. Bibl. Nat. Paris Arch. E.R.L.

69 1. Claude Monet: *The Magpie,* 1867. S.b.r. (0.89 × 1.30). Private Coll. D.R. © Spadem 1983.
2. Claude Monet: *Road to Saint-Siméon Farm in the Snow,* 1867 (0.56 × 0.81). Louvre, Paris. S.b.l. Ph. Giraudon. © Spadem 1983.
3. Ph. Arch. E.R.L.

70 1. Gustave Courbet: *The Mouth of the Seine,* c. 1841 (0.43 × 0.65). S.b.l. Musée des Beaux-Arts, Lille.
2. Ph. N.D. Arch. E.R.L.
3. Camille Corot: *Calvary on the Grace Coast, Honfleur,* c. 1830. Private coll. D.R.
4. Ph. Bibl. Nat. Paris.
5. Georges Braque: *Grace Coast at Honfleur,* 1905. S.b.l. (0.62 × 0.50). Musée des Beaux-Arts Le Havre. Bought by the city, 1930. © Adagp 1983.

71 1. Henri-Charles Manguin: *Honfleur, View of the Grace Coast,* 1910 (0.22 × 0.27). S.b.l. Coll. Mme Manguin © Adagp 1983.
2. Félix Vallotton: *Honfleur and the bay of the Seine. Grey evening,* 1910 (0.88 × 0.82). Family journal N° 740. Coll. Galerie Vallotton, Lausanne. © Spadem 1983.

72 1. Ph. Arch. E.R.L.
2. Ph. G. Demais. E.R.L.
3. Gustave Courbet: *Portrait of Baudelaire,* 1845-50 (0.53 × 0.61). Musée Fabre, Montpellier. Ph. Giraudon.
4. Claude Monet: *Rue de la Bavolle, Honfleur,* c. 1866 (0.34 × ·0.61). Museum of Fine Arts Boston, Gift of John T. Spauldind © Spadem 1983.

73 1. Ph. Arch. E.R.L.
2. Johan Barthold Jongkind: *Sainte Catherine, Honfleur,* 1864. Watercolor. S.D.b.l. (0.365 × 0.435). Musée des Arts Décoratifs Paris. Ph. Roger-Viollet.
3. Attributed to Claude Monet: *The Steeple of Sainte Catherine,* c. 1867. Oil on wood (0.55 × 0.43). S.b.l. Musée Eugène-Boudin, Honfleur. Gift of M. Monet. Ph. G. Demais. E.R.L. © Spadem 1983.
4. Johan Bathold Jongkind: *Street in Honfleur,* 1863. S.D.b.r. (0.42 × 0.57). Robert Schmit Collection, Paris.

74 1. Louis-Alexandre Dubourg: *Bathing at Honfleur,* 1869 (0.50 × 0.86). S.b.r. Musée Eugène Boudin, Honfleur. Ph. Schuller.
2. Ph. Roger-Viollet.
3. Ph. Arch. E.R.L.
4. Louis-Alexandre Dubourg: *Beach at Honfleur,* (0.244 × 0.445). Musée Eugène-Boudin, Honfleur. Legs D. Louveau. Ph. G. Demais. E.R.L.

75 1. Bibl. Nat. Paris.
2. Ph. N.D. Arch. E.R.L.
3. Georges Seurat: *The Maria, Honfleur,* 1886 (0.54 × 0.64). S.b.r. National Gallery Prague. Ph. Giraudon.
4. Claude Monet: *Lighthouse at Honfleur,* 1864. Private Coll. Ph. Giraudon © Spadem 1983.

76 1. Louis-Alexandre Dubourg: *Honfleur Pier,* 1870 (0.50 × 0.80). S.b.r. Musée Eugène-Boudin, Honfleur. Ph. G. Demais, E.R.L.
2. Ph. Arch. E.R.L.
3. Johan Barthold Jongkind: *Port of Honfleur,* 1866. S.D.b.l. (0.42 × 0.56). Louvre, Paris. Don E. & V. Lyon. Ph. Réunion des Musées Nat.
4. Louis-Alexandre Dubourg: *Sail boats.* Musée Eugène-Boudin, Honfleur. Ph. G. Demais E.R.L.

77 1. Ph. Bibl. Nat. Paris.
2. Johan Barthold Jongkind: *Thatched Cottage,* Graphite on paper. S.b.l. (14.5 × 22.5). Musée des Beaux-Arts Besançon.
3. Ph. Robert Demachy. S.F.P.
4. Eugène Boudin: *Cows near the Sea,* c. 1890-97. Oil on wood (0.54 × 0.74). Musée des Beaux-Arts, Le Havre. Legs L. Boudin. Ph. G. Demais E.R.L.

78 1. Eugène Boudin:; *Women and Children in front of Trouville Casino,* c. 1874. Oil on wooden panel (0.22 × 0.12). Musée Eugène-Boudin, Honfleur. Legs Eugène Boudin. Ph. G. Demais E.R.L.
2. Ph. Collection Sirot-Angel.
3. Ph. Collection Sirot-Angel.
4. Eugène Boudin painting on the boardwalk at Deauville. Photo dedicated to Goerges Sporck, 1896. Musée Eugène-Boudin Honfleur.
5. Eugène Boudin: *Beach at Trouville,* 1876. S.b.l. Oil on wooden panel (0.12 × 0.25). Musée Eugène-Boudin, Honfleur. Ph. G. Demais E.R.L.

79 1. Claude Monet: *Camille Monet and her Cousin on the Beach at Trouville,* 1870 (0.38 × 0.46). S.b.l. Musée Marmatton, Paris. Ph. Studio Lourmel. © Spadem 1983.

80-81. Eugène Boudin: *The Beach at Trouville,* 1863. S.D.b.l. Oil on wood (0.346 × 0.568). National Gallery of Art, Washington D.C.

82 1. Autochrome. Coll. S.F.P. Fotogram.
2. Eugène Boudin: *Woman with Parosal on the beach at Trouville,* c. 1880. Oil on wooden panel (0.125 × 0.175). Musée Eugène-Boudin, Honfleur. Legs Eugène Boudin. Ph. G. Demais E.R.L.

83 1. Eugène Boudin: *Beach at Trouville.* Musée des Beaux-Arts, Reims. Ph. E.R.L.
2. Ph. N.D. E.R.L.
3. Ph. Arch. E.R.L.

84 1. Eugène Isabey: *The Rocks at Etretat,* 1857. Watercolor and gouache. S.D.b.r. (0.24 × 0.33). Louvre, Paris. Ph. Réunion des Musées Nat.
2. Gustave Courbet: *Cliffs at Etretat after Storm,* 1870. S.b.l. (1.33 × 1.62). Louvre, Paris. Ph. Réunion des Musées Nat.
3. Ph. Bibl. Nat. Paris.
4. Ph. Bibl. Nat. Paris.

85 1. Eugène Boudin: *Cliffs at Etretat,* c. 1890-94. Oil on wood (0.38 × 0.47). Musée des Beaux-Arts, Le Havre. Don Eugène Boudin. Ph. G. Demais E.R.L.
2. Claude Monet: *Etretat. Rough Sea,* 1883. S.D.b.l. (0.81 × 1.00). Musée des Beaux-Arts, Lyon. Ph. B. Lontin. © Spadem 1983.

86 1. Gustave Courbet: *Honfleur Estuary* (0.326 × 0.410). S.b.l. Musée Eugène-Boudin. Don Katia Granoff. Ph. G. Demais E.R.L.
2. Ph. Arch. E.R.L.
3. Édouard Manet: *Boats at Sunset,* 1872-73 (0.42 × 0.94). Musée des Beaux-Arts, Le Havre. Ph. G. Demais E.R.L.

87 1. Ph. Arch. E.R.L.
2. Charles-François Daubigny: *Sunset.* A. Watteau Coll. Neuilly-sur-Seine.
3. Eugène Boudin: *Twilight at Le Havre Docks,* c. 1892-94. Oil on wood (0.40 × 0.65). Musée des Beaux-Arts, Le Havre. Don L. Boudin, 1900. Ph. G. Demais. E.R.L.

88 1. Claude Monet: *Terrace at Ste-Adresse,* 1867. S.D.b.r. (0.98 × 1.30). Metropolitan Museum of Art, New York. © Spadem 1983.
2. Ph. Roger-Viollet.

89 1. Claude Monet: *Impression, Sunset,* 1872. S.D.b.l. (0.48 × 0.63). Musée Marmottan, Paris. Ph. Routhier. © Spadem 1983.
2. Édouard Manet: *Portrait of Monet,* 1874. Chinese ink wash (0.18 × 0.14). Musée Marmottan, Paris. Ph. Studio Lourmel.
3. Ph. Arch. E.R.L.

90 1. Raoul Dufy: *The Beach at Ste Adresse,* 1904 (0.65 × 0.81). S.b.l. Musée Nat. d'Art Moderne. C.N.A.C., Paris. © Spadem 1983.
2. Ph. Arch. E.R.L.
3. Albert Marquet: *The Beach at Ste dresse,* 1906 (0.38 × 0.81). S.b.l. Private Coll. Paris. Ph. Giraudon © Adagp 1983.

91 1. Albert Marquet: *Outer Harbor at Le Havre.* S.b.r. Musée des Beaux-Arts, Le Havre. Ph. G. Demais. E.R.L.
2. Ph. Arch. E.R.L.

92 1. Claude Monet: *La Grenouillère,* 1869. Detail (see p. 103). Metropolitan Museum, New York. Gift of Mrs H.O. Havemeyer, 1929. © Spadem 1983.

93 1. Édouard Manet: *Claude Monet in his Studio,* 1874 (0.82 × 1.04). Neue Pinakothek, Munich.

98 1. Charles Daubigny: *The Departure.* Pen and ink (0.11 × 0.16). Louvre, Paris. Cbt des Dessins. Ph. Réunion des Musées Nat.
2. Gustave Courbet: *Young Women on the bank of the Seine,* 1856-57 (1.74 × 2.00). S.b.l. Musée du Petit-Palais, Paris. Ph. Giraudon.
3. Giorgione: *Le Concert Champêtre.* Detail. Louvre, Paris. Ph. Giraudon.
4. Marcantonuo Raimondi: *Judgement of Paris.* Detail. Ph. Giraudon.
5. Frédéric Bazille: *Family Reunion,* 1867 (1.52 × 2.30). S.D.b.l. Louvre, Paris. Ph. Réunion des Musées Nat.

99 1. Édouard Manet: *Luncheon on the Grass,* 1862-63 (2.08 × 2.64). S.D.b.r. Musée du Jeu de Paume, Paris. Ph. Réunion des Musées Nat.
2. Paul Cézanne: *Luncheon on the Grass,* 1873 (0.21 × 0.26). Louvre, Paris. Coll. Paul Guillaume-Jean Walter. Ph. Réunion des Musées Nat.

100 1. Pierre-Auguste Renoir: *La Grenouillère,* 1869 (0.66 × 0.81). S.b.l. National Museum Stockholm. © Spadem 1983.

101 1. Oreste Cortazzo: *La Grenouillère.* Woodcut illustration for G. de Maupassant's "Yvette". Bibl. Nat. Paris. Arch. E.R.L.
2. Ph. Collection Debuisson.
3. Édouard Riou: *Paris in the Country. La Grenouillère,* 1868. S.b.l. Ph. Bibl. Nat. Paris.

102 1. Ph. Collection Debuisson.
2. Ferdinand Lunel: *La Grenouillère,* 1885. S.b.r. Bibl. Nat. Paris. Arch. E.R.L.
3. Paul Destez: *The Thursday Evening Dance at La Grenouillère.* 1885. S.b.l. Bibl. Nat. Paris. Arch. E.R.L.

103 1. Claude Monet: *La Grenouillère,* 1869 (0.746 × 0.997). S.b.r. Metropolitan Museum of Art, New York. © Spadem 1983.
2. Sketch representing summer at Bougival. 1859. Bibl. Nat. Paris. Arch. E.R.L.
3. Miranda: *La Grenouillère on Croissy Island,* 1869. S.b.r. Bibl. Nat. Paris.

104 1. Ph. S.F.P.
2. Gustave Caillebotte: *Rower in Top Hat,* 1879 (0.90 × 1.17). S.b.r. Private collection. Ph. Fondation Wildenstein.
3. Ph. N.D. Arch. E.R.L.
4. Claude Monet: *Boating on the River Epte,* 1890 (1.33 × 1.45). Coll. Museum of Art Saõ Paulo, Brazil. © Spadem 1983.
5. Ph. Arch. E.R.L.
6. Pierre-Auguste Renoir: *Edmond Renoir Fishing.* Pen and ink drawing (0.20 × 0.31). Private Coll. Viroflay. © Spadem 1983.

105 1. Édouard Manet: *Argenteuil,* 1874 (1.49 × 1.15). S.D.b.r. Musée des Beaux-Arts de Tournai. Bequest H. van Custem. Ph. E. Lessing-Magnum.
2. Ph. Jacques Guignard, Chatou.

106 1. Edmond Morin: *Restaurant 'Matelote and Fritures',* July 1877.
2. Pierre-Auguste Renoir: *The Seine at Argenteuil,* 1873 (0.50 × 0.65). S.b.r. The Portland Art Museum. Gift of Winslow B. Ayer. © Spadem 1983.
3. Ph. Author's Collection.
4. Édouard Manet: *Boating,* 1874 (0.97 × 1.30). S.b.r. Metropolitan Museum New York. Gift Mrs. H.O. Havemeyer, 1929.

107 1. Georges Seurat: *The Seine at Grande Jatte, Spring,* 1887 (0.65 × 0.81). S.b.r. Musées Royaux des Beaux-Arts, Brussels.
2. Ph. Author's Collection.
3. Gustave Caillebotte: *Sailboats at Argenteuil,* 1888 (0.65 × 0.55). S.b.r. Musée du Jeu de Paume, Paris. Ph. Réunion des Musées Nat.

108 1. John Sargent: *Claude Monet Painting,* 1887. Tate Gallery, London.
2. Autochrome. Collection Personnaz. S.F.P. Fotogram.
3. Claude Monet: *Field of Poppies,* 1873 (0.50 × 0.65). S.D.b.l. Musée du Jeu de

Paume, Paris. Ph. E.R.L. © Spadem 1983.
4. Pierre-Auguste Renoir: *Portrait of Berthe Morisot*. Ph. Bibl. Nat. Paris. © Spadem 1983.
5. Berthe Morisot: *The Butterfly Chase* (0.46 × 0.56). S.b.r. Musée du Jeu de Paume, Paris. Arch. E.R.L.

109 1. Camille Pissarro: *The Lock*, 1872 (0.53 × 0.83). S.D.b.r. Ph. Durand-Ruel, Paris.
2. Ph. Reader's Digest selection.
3. Alfred Sisley: *Boat at Bougival Lock*, 1873 (0.47 × 0.65). S.D.b.r. Musée du Jeu de Paume, Paris. Arch. E.R.L.

110 1. Ph. Bibl. Nat. Paris. Arch. E.R.L.
2. Ph. Jacques Guignard Collection, Chatou.
3. Ph. Arch. E.R.L.
4. Pierre-Auguste Renoir: *Railroad Bridge at Chatou*, 1881 (0.540 × 0.657). S.D.b.r. Musée du Jeu de Paume, Paris. Arch. E.R.L. © Spadem 1983.

111 1. Pierre-Auguste Renoir: *Alphonse Fournaise*, 1879, Christiane Parère Collection. © Spadem 1983.
2. Pierre-Auguste Renoir: *The Boatmens Lunch*, 1881 (0.72 × 1.27). S.D.b.r. Phillips Collection, Washington. © Spadem 1983.
3. Pierre-Auguste Renoir: *Alphonsine Fournaise*, 1879. Christiane Parère Collection. © Spadem 1983.

112 1. Ph. Arch. E.R.L.
2. Pierre Puvis de Chavannes: *Hope* (2nd version) (0.70 × 0.82). S.b.l. Ph. Réunion des Musées Nat.
3. Frédéric Bazille: *Summer Scene, Bathers*, 1869 (1.58 × 1.58). S.D.b.l. Fogg Art Museum Cambridge, Mass. Gift of Mr. and Mrs. F. Meynier de Salinelles.
4. Ph. Robert Demachy. S.F.P.

113 1. Autochrome. Collection Personnaz. S.F.P. Fotogram.
2. Georges Seurat: *Bathers, Asnières*, 1883-84 (2.01 × 3.01). S.b.l. National Gallery, London. Ph. E. Tweedy.

114 1. Gustave Caillebotte: *The Diver*, 1877 (0.72 × 0.92). S.c.r. Musée Municipal d'Agen. Ph. Giraudon.
2. Ph. Jacques Guignard Collection, Chatou.
3. Mary Cassatt: *Bathing* (1.29 × 0.99). S.b.r. Musée du Petit-Palais, Paris. Ph. Giraudon. © Adagp 1983.
4. Anthony Morlon: *Bathing Party at Bougival*. Bibl. Nat. Paris Arch. E.R.L.
5. Félix Vallotton: *The Source*, 1897. Oil on cardboard (0.48 × 0.60). S.D.b.r. Musée du Petit-Palais, Geneva. © Spadem 1983.

115 1. Pierre-Auguste Renoir: *Bathers*, 1887 (1.07 × 1.70). S.D.b.r. Philadelphia Museum of Art. Tyson Collection. Ph. Edimedia. © Spadem 1983.
2. François Girardon: *Nymphs Bathing*, Low relief. North section of pont in the gardens at Versailles. Ph. Giraudon.
3. Pierre-Auguste Renoir: *Young Bather*, 1892. S.D.b.l. Lehmann Collection. Ph. Giraudon. © Spadem 1983.

116 1. Alfred Sisley: *Flood at Pont-Marly*, 1876 (0.505 × 0.610). S.D.b.r. Musée du Jeu de Paume, Paris. Arch. E.R.L.
2. Claude Monet: *Vétheuil in Summer*, 1880 (0.60 × 0.99). S.D.b.r. Metropolitan Museum, New York. Gift of Mr. William Church Osborn, 1951. © Spadem 1983.
3. Ph. Roger-Viollet.

117 1. Ph. J. Warnod Coll.
2. Georges Seurat: *Sunday Afternoon on the Island of La Grande Jatte*, 1884-86 (2.05 × 3.05). The Art Institute of Chicago, Helen Birch Bartlett Mem. Coll.
3. Ph. Arch. E.R.L.
4. Paul Signac: *Woman with Parasol*, 1893. S.D.b.l. JH. Warnod Collection.

118-119 Georges Seurat: *Sunday Afternoon on the Island of La Grande Jatte*, 1884-86 (2.05 × 3.05). The Art Institute of Chicago. Helen Birch Bartlett Mem. Coll.

120 1. Vincent Van Gogh: *Restaurant de la Sirène*, 1887 (0.515 × 0.640). Ashmolean Museum, Oxford.
2. Ph. Stedelijk Museum, Amsterdam.
3. Ph. Collection Debuisson.
4. Vincent Van Gogh: *Bateau Lavoir* (Asnières), 1887 (0.19 × 0.26). Coll. Mr. and Mrs. Paul Mellon, Upperville, U.S.A.

121 1. Émile Bernard: *The Asnières Bridge*, 1887 (0.45 × 0.54). S.D.b.r. Museum of Modern Art, New York, Fond. Grace Raincy Rogers.
2. Ph. Roger-Viollet.
3. Vincent Van Gogh: *Asnières Bridge*, 1887 (50.52 × 0.65). Stiftung Sammlung E.G. Bührle, Zurich. Ph. A. Held-Ziolo.

122 1. Charles Daubigny: *Washerwomen on the shores of the River Oise*, c. 1855. Oil on panel (0.21 × 0.35). S.b.r. Coll. J.C.P.B., Paris.
2. Léonide Bourges: *Daubigny. Memoires and Sketches*. Coll. private D.R.
3. Camille Pissarro: *Portrait of Cézanne*, Bibl. Nat. Paris.
4. Vincent Van Gogh: *Portrait of Doctor Gachet*, 1890 (0.68 × 0.57). Musée du Jeu de Paume, Paris. Ph. Réunion des Musées Nat.

123 1. Paul Cézanne: *Cézanne Engraving Near Dr. Gachet*, 1873. Graphite on yellowed paper (0.204 × 0.132). Arch. E.R.L.
2. Ph. Stedelijk Museum, Amsterdam.
3. Paul Cézanne: *The House of Dr. Gachet*, 1873-74 (0.56 × 0.47). Kunstmuseum, Basel. Ph. Hinz.

124 1. Vincent Van Gogh: *Daubigny's Garden*, 1890 (0.65 × 0.01). Rudolphe Staechelin Coll. Basel. Ph. Hinz.
2. Léonide Bourges: *Charles Daubigny*. S.b.r. Bibl. Nat. Paris.
3. Vincent Van Gogh: *Stairway at Auvers*, 1890 (0.51 × 0.71). Saint Louis City Art Museum.
4. Ph. G. Demais. E.R.L.

125 1. Ph. Roger-Viollet.
2. Paul Cézanne: *The House of the Hanged Man*, 1872-73 (0.55 × 0.66). S.b.r. Musée du Jeu de Paume, Paris. Camondo Donation. Arch. E.R.L.
3. Vincent Van Gogh: *The Church at Auvers*, 1890 (0.94 × 0.74). Musée du Jeu de Paume, Paris, Ph. Réunion des Musées Nat.

126 1. Vincent Van Gogh: *At the Bar*, 1890. Graphite sketch (0.13 × 0.33). Coll. Ed. Buckman, Richmond.
2. Ph. Stedelijk Museum, Amsterdam.
3. Vincent Van Gogh: *Portrait of Adeline Ravoux*, 1890 (0.67 × 0.55). Coll. J.R. Oppenheimer, New York.
4. Jean-François Millet: *Crows in Winter*, 1866 (0.60 × 0.73). S.b.r. Kunsthistorisches Museum, Vienna.
5. Charles Daubigny: *Tree with Crows*, 1867. Etching (0.278 × 1.83). Arch. E.R.L.
6-7. Ph. Stedelijk Museum, Amsterdam.

127 1. Vincent Van Gogh: *Crows over a Wheatfield*, 1890 (0.505 × 1.105). Vincent Van Gogh Museum, Amsterdam.
2. Ph. G. Demais. E.R.L.
3. Vincent Van Gogh: *The Garden of Dr. Gachet*, 1890 (0.730 × 5.15). Louvre, Paris. Ph. Giraudon.

128 1. Joseph Mallord William Turner: *The facade of Rouen Cathedral*, 1832. Watercolor and gouache on blue paper (0.140 × 0.194). British Museum, London. Ph. E. Tweedy.
2. Lucien Pissarro: *Camille Pissarro*. Drawing. S.b.r. Bibl. Nat. Paris.
3. Ph. Roger-Viollet.
4. Camille Pissarro: *The Boïeldieu Bridge at Rouen*, 1896 (0.737 × 0.914). S.D.b.r. Art Gallery of Ontario, Toronto. Gift of Reuben Wells Leonard Estate.

129 1. Claude Monet: *Rouen Cathedral. Blue Harmony*, 1894 (0.91 × 0.63). S.D.b.r. Musée du Jeu de Paume, Paris. Arch. E.R.L. © Spadem 1983.
2. Ph. Departmental archives of Seine-Maritime.
3. Claude Monet: *Rouen Cathedral. White Harmony*, 1894 (1.06 × 0.73). S.D.b.r. Musée du Jeu de Paume, Paris. Arch. E.R.L. © Spadem 1983.
4. Camille Pissarro: *The Old Market at Rouen*, 1898 (0.913 × 0.651). S.D.b.l. Metropolitan Museum of Art, New York. Gift of Mr. & Mrs. Richard J. Berhnard.

130 1. *Illustration*, November 4, 1905. Author's collection.
2. Henri Rousseau: *The Hungry Lion*... Detail (2.00 × 2.00). S.b.r. Private coll. Switzerland. Photo H. Hinz.
3. Ph. J. Tribondeau, 1955.

131 1. Maurice de Vlaminck: *The Chatou Bridge*, 1906 (0.54 × 0.73). S.b.l. Musée de l'Annonciade, Saint-Tropez (legs Grammont, 1955). Ph. Giraudon. © Spadem 1983.
2. Ph. Bibl. Nat. Paris. Arch. E.R.L.
3. Photo, 1899. Jacques Guignard Coll. Chatou.
4. André Derain: *The Seine at Chatou*, 1904 (0.605 × 0.735). S.b.r. Stedelijk Museum, Amsterdam. © Adagp 1983.

132 1. Camille Camoin: *Portrait of Albert Marquet*, 1904 (0.92 × 0.73). S.b.l. Musée d'Art Moderne, Paris. Gift of Mrs. Marquet, 1948. Ph. Giraudon. © Adagp 1983.
2. André Derain: *Portrait of Maurice Vlaminck*, 1905. Coll. Mrs. Vlaminck. Ph. Giraudon. © Spadem 1983.
3. André Derain: *Portrait of Henri Matisse*, 1905 (0.460 × 0.349). S.b.r. The Tate Gallery, London. © Adagp 1983.
4. Henri Matisse: *Portrait of André Derain*, 1905. Initials b.r. The Tate Gallery, London. © Spadem 1983.

133 1. Henri Matisse: *Le Luxe I*, 1907 (2.10 × 1.38). Initials b.r. Musée National d'Art Moderne, Paris. Ph. J. Guillot. Edimedia. © Spadem 1983.

134 1. Claude Monet: *Bridge over Waterlily Pond*, 1899 (0.927 × 0.737). S.D.b.r. Metropolitan Museum of Art. Gift of Mrs. H.O. Havemeyer, 1929. © Spadem 1983.
2. Claude Monet: *Flowered Arches*, Giverny, 1912 (0.806 × 0.800). S.b.l. Phœnix Art Museum. Gift of Mr. and Mrs. Donald D. Harrington. © Spaden 1983.
3. Ph. 1902. Ph. Piguet Coll.
4. Ph. Mme Verneiges Coll.

135 1. Claude Monet: *Waterlilies; Water landscapes*, 1905 (0.895 × 0.996). S.D.b.r. Museum of Fine Arts, Boston. Gift of Edward Jackson Holmes. © Spadem 1983,
2. Photo. Ph. Piguet Coll.
3. Ph. Bulloz.

136 1. Henri de Toulouse-Lautrec: *The Dance at the Moulin Rouge*, 1890. Detail (see p. 163). Coll. Mr. Henry P. McIlhenny, Philadelphia. Ph. Fabbri Editore.

137 1. Henri de Toulouse-Lautrec: *Artist Painting*, 1884 (0.51 × 0.43). Stamped b.l. Coll. Musée du Prieuré, St-Germain-en-Laye.

142 1. Édourd Manet: *Portrait of Émile Zola*, 1868. Musée du Jeu de Paume, Paris, Ph. E.R.L.
2. Ph. Bibl. Nat. Paris. Arch. E.R.L.
3. JPh. Coll. Sirot-Angel.
4. Henri Fantin-Latour: *Studio at Batignolles*, 1870 (2.04 × 2.70). Left to right: O. Scholderer, Manet, Renoir, Z. Astruc, Zola, E. Maître, Bazille, Monet. Jeu de Paume, Paris. Ph. E.R.L.

143 1. Ph. Bibl. Nat. Paris. Arch. E.R.L.
2. *Henri de Toulouse-Lautrec by Henri de Toulouse-Lautrec*, 1896. Pencil drawing (0.10 × 0.09). Musée Henri de Toulouse-Lautrec, Albi. Arch. E.R.L.
3. Phot. 1885. J. Warnod Coll.
4. Ph. 1890. Bibl. Nat. Paris.

144 1. Frédéric Bazille: *Painter's Studio*, 1870 (0.99 × 1.20). S.D.b.r. Louvre, Paris. Ph. Giraudon.
2. Pierre-Auguste Renoir: *Artists Studio at Rue St. Georges*, 1876 (0.45 × 0.37). S.b.r. Left to right: Lestringuez, Rivière, Pissarro, the musician Cabaner, at the back Cordey. Coll. Sotheby's Press Office, London. © Spadem 1983.
3. Edouard Vuillard: *Portrait of Thadée Natanson*, 1908. Tempera on canvas (2 × 2). S.b.r. Musée d'Art Moderne, Paris. Legs Mme Reine Thadée Natanson. Ph. Giraudon. © Spadem 1983.
4. Armand Guillaumin: *Martinez in Guillaumin's Studio*, 1878 (0.85 × 0.73). S.b.r. Coll. Mr. & Mrs. Paul Mellon, Upperville. U.S.A. © Adagp 1983.
5. Photo. end of 19th century. Arch. E.R.L.

145 1. Phot. 1900-1910. Arch. E.R.L.
2. Photo Arch. E.R.L.
3. Maximilien Luce: *Suzanne Valadon's House, Montmartre*, 1895 (0.54 × 0.65). S.D.b.r. Coll. M. Gerald Cantoz. U.S.A. Ph. Bibl. des Arts, Lausanne. × Spadem 1983.
4. Suzanne Valdadon: *Rue Cortot*. S.b.r. Musée des Beaux-Arts, Alger. Arch. E.R.L. © Spadem 1983.

146 1. Gustave Caillebotte: *At the Café*, 1880 (1.53 × 1.14). S.D.b.r. Musée des Beaux-Arts, Rouen. Arch. E.R.L.
2. Édouard Manet: *The Beer-waitress*, c. 1878-1879 (0.775 × 0.650). Jeu de Paume, Paris. Ph. Giraudon.
3. Édouard Manet: *Café*, 1869. Ink on paper (0.295 × 0.403). Fogg Art Museum, Cambridge, Ma. Coll. Paul J. Sachs. Arch. E.R.L.
4. Jean-Louis Forain: *At the Café*. S.t.r. Louvre, Paris. Cbt. des dessins. © Spadem 1983.
5. Ph. Roger-Viollet.

147 1. Édouard Manet: *At Père Lathuille's*, 1879 (0.920 × 1.120). S.D.b.l. Musée des Beaux-Arts, Tournai. Legs M. H. van Cutsemqui. Ph. Studio Gamma. S.P.R.L.
2. Frédéric Regamey: *Gervaise and Coupeau*. Illustration for Zola's *The Dram-Shop*, 1878. Bibl. Nat. Paris. Arch. E.R.L.
3. Ph. Coll. Sirot-Angel.
4. Edgar Degas: *Women on a café terrace* (Blvd. Montmartre). 1877 (0.40 × 0.60). Musée du Jeu de Paume, Paris. Ph. Réunion des Musées Nat. © Spadem 1983.

148 1. Édouard Manet: *The Plum*, 1877 (0.74 × 0.49). National Gallery of Art, Washington. Mr. and Mrs. Paul Mellon Collection.
2. Ellen Andrée model for Degas's *Absinthe*. Ph. Coll. Sirot-Angel.
3. Ph. Coll. Sirot-Angel.

149 1. Edgar Degas: *Absinthe*, 1876 (M. Desboutin and E. Andrée) (0.92 × 0.68). S.b.l. Musée du Jeu de Paume, Paris. Ph. Giraudon. © Spadem 1983.
2. Ph. Bibl. Nat. Paris.
3. Edgard Degas: *The Café de la Nouvelle Athènes*, 1878. Pencil. Arch. E.R.L. © Spadem 1983.
4. Henri de Toulouse-Lautrec: *The Drinker or Hangover*, 1889. Chinese ink and blue pencil (0.48 × 0.63). S.b.r. Musée Henri de Toulouse-Lautrec, Albi. Ph. Giraudon.
5. Federico Zandomeneghi: *At the Café de la Nouvelle Athènes*, 1885 (Self portrait with Suzanne Valadon). S.D.b.r. Coll. Piero Dini, Italy.

150 1. Ph. Coll. Sirot-Angel.
2. Henri de Toulouse-Lautrec: *Yvette Cuilbert Taking a Curtain Call*, 1894. Musée Henri de Toulouse-Lautrec, Albi. Ph. Giraudon.
3. Edgar Degas: *Café Singer*, 1878 (0.53 × 0.41). S.t.l. Fogg Art Museum, Cambridge, Ma. Bequest of Coll. Maurice Wertheil. © Spadem 1983.
4. Henri de Toulouse-Lautrec: *The Divan Japonais*, 1892. Poster. S.b.r. Ph. Giraudon.
5. Ferdinand Lunel: *The Divan Japonais, rue des Martyrs*, 1889. Coll. Romi.

151 1. Henri Somm: *Illustrated Menu for the Rat Mort*, July 1, 1894. Bibl. Nat. Paris Arch. E.R.L.
2. Honoré Daumier: *The Café Concert*. Arch. E.R.L.
3. Maurice de Vlaminck: *Dancer from the Rat Mort Cabaret*, 1906 (0.73 × 0.54). Private Coll. Ph. Giraudon. © Spadem 1983.

152 1. Pierre-Auguste Renoir: *Country Dance*, 1882-83 (1.80 × 0.90). S.D.b.l. Musée du Jeu de Paume, Paris. Ph. H. Hosse. © Spadem 1983.
2. Ph. Roger-Viollet.
3. Théophile Steinlen: *The 14th of July Dance*. Private coll. Ph. Giraudon. © Spadem 1983.

153 1. Edgar Degas: *At the Café Concert*, 1875-77 (0.55 × 0.45). S.b.r. Havemeyer Coll. New York. Sotheby's document.

154-155 Pierre-Auguste Renoir: *The Moulin de la Galette*, 1876 (1.31 × 1.75). S.b.r. Louvre, Paris. Arch. E.R.L. © Spadem 1983.
2. Frédéric Bazille: *Portrait of Renoir*, 1867 (0.61 × 0.50). Musée du Jeu de Paume, Paris. Ph. Giraudon.

156 1. Vincent Van Gogh: *Le Moulin de la Galette*, 1886 (0.380 × 0.465). Nationalgalerie, Berlin. Ph. Jorg P. Anders.
2. Ph. Seeberger.
3. Ph. J. Warnod Coll.

157 1. Ph. E.R.L.
2. Théophile Steinlen: *Windmills in Montmartre,* 1903 (0.66 × 0.95). Musée du Petit Palais, Geneva. © Spadem 1983.
3. Maurice Utrillo: *The Moulin de la Galette,* 1913-15 (0.280 × 0.445). S.b.r. Villert. Private coll. Ph. A. Held-Ziolo. © Spadem 1983.
4. Marcel Leprin: *The Moulin de la Galette, 1918.* Oil on cardboard (0.52 × 0.68). Musée du Petit Palais, Geneva. © Spadem 1983.
158 1. Roedel: *Poster for the Moulin de la Galette.* Coll. Romi.
2. Ph. Drouillet, 1904. Coll. Sirot-Angel.
3. Federico Zandemeneghi: *The Moulin de la Galette,* 1878-79 (0.80 × 1.10). S.b.r. Coll. M.G. Piceni, Milan.
4. Pablo Picasso: *The Moulin de la Galette,* 1900 (0.902 × 1.170). S.b.r. Private coll. Ph. Giraudon. © Spadem 1983.
159 1. Henri de Toulouse-Lautrec: *Dance at the Moulin de la Galette,* 1889 (0.980 × 0.102). S.b.l. Art Institute Chicago. Mr. & Mrs. L. Coburn coll.
2. Musée Montmartre, Paris. Ph. E.R.L.
3. Kees Van Dongen: *The Moulin de la Galette,* 1904 (0.65 × 0.54). S.b.l. Musée d'Art Moderne, Troyes. Donation Pierre Lévy. © Spadem 1983.
160 1. Henri de Toulouse-Lautrec: *Poster for Jardin de Paris,* 1893 (1.30 × 0.95). S.D.b.l. Bibl. Nat. Paris. Ph. Giraudon.
2. Ph. Bibl. Nat. Paris.
3. Ph. Coll. Sirot-Angel.
4. Georges Redon: *The Place Blanche; The Evening of the Dance,* 1891. Bibl. Nat. Paris.
161 1. Pablo Picasso: *Self Portrait in front of The Moulin Rouge,* 1901. Ink and colored pencil on paper (0.180 × 0.115). S.b.r. Coll. Mrs. E. Heywood Lonsdale, London. Arch. E.R.L. © Spadem 1983.
2. Auguste Chabaud: *The Moulin Rouge at Night,* 1905. Oil on cardboard (0.82 × 0.60). S.b.r. Galerie Beyeler, Basel. Ph. A. Held-Ziolo. © Adagp 1983.
162 1. Henri de Toulouse-Lautrec: *Mlle Eglantine's Dancers* (Églantine, Jane Avril, Cleopatra, Gazelle). 1896 (0.61 × 0.78). S.b.l. Musée de Henri de Toulouse-Lautrec, Albi.
2. Henri de Toulouse-Lautrec: *The Gouloue Entering the Moulin Rouge,* 1891-92 (0.794 × 0.590). S.b.l. Museum of Modern Art, New York. Lévy Donation.
3. Ph. Bacard Fils: La Gouloue and Grille d'Egout. Arch. E.R.L.
4. Can-can Dancers at the Moulin Rouge: *La Sauterelle, Nini Pattes en l'air, La Gouloue, Môme Fromage, Grille d'Égout.* Ph. Coll. Sirot-Angel.
163 1. Photo, 1900 Coll. René Dazy.
2. Henri de Toulouse-Lautrec: *The Dance at the Moulin Rouge,* 1890 (1.155 × 1.500). Coll. Mr. & Mrs. H.P. McIlhenny, Philadelphia. Ph. Fabbri Editore.
164 1. Photo 1900. Bibl. Nat. Paris. Arch. E.R.L.
2. Pierre Bonnard: *Poster for France Champagne,* 1889. J. Warnod Coll. © Adagp 1983.
165 1. Édouard Manet: *The Bar at the Folies-Bergère,* 1881 (0.96 × 1.30). Courtauld Institute Galleries, London. Ph. The Bridgeman Art Library.
166 1. Maximilien Luce: *Rue des Abbesses,* 1896 (0.54 × 0.75). S.D.b.l. Musée du Petit Palais, Geneva. © Spadem 1983.
2. Pierre Bonnard: *Woman with Umbrella,* 1900 (0.63 × 0.43). S.b.l. Private coll. Arch. E.R.L. © Adagp 1983.
3. Musée Montmartre. Ph. E.R.L.
4. Félix Vallotton: *The Downpour,* 1894 (0.227 × 0.313). Initials D.b.r. Private Coll. © Spadem 1983.
5. Théophile Steinlen: *Carriages,* J. Warnod Coll. © Spadem 1983.
167 1. Jean-François Raffaelli: *Boulevard des Italiens,* (0.635 × 1.085). S.b.r. Ph. Galerie Daniel Malingue, Paris.
2. Ph. Coll. René Jacques.
3. Ph. Roger-Viollet.
4. Camille Pissarro: *Boulevard Montmartre,* 1897 (0,73 × 0.92). S.D.b.r. Hermitage Museum, Leningrad.
168 1. Henri de Toulouse-Lautrec: *The Salon at Rue ses Moulins,* 1894 (1.115 × 1.325). Monogram b.l. Musée de Henri de Toulouse-Lautrec, Albi. Ph. Giraudon.
2. Edgar Degas: *Waiting* (From the *Maisons Closes* series). Monotype in black ink on Chinese paper (0.216 × 0.164). Coll. Romi. © Spadem 1983.
3. Edgar Degas: *The Client* (from the *Maisons Closes* series). Monotype in black ink on Chinese paper (0.216 × 0.164). Coll. Romi. © Spadem 1983.
169 1. Photo. 1894. Coll. Edimédia.
2. Ph. J. Warnod Collection.
3. Henri de Toulouse-Lautrec: *The Inhabitants of rue des Moulins,* 1894. Private Coll. Arch. E.R.L.
4. Georges Rouält: *Girl at the Mirror,* 1906. Watercolor on cardboard (0.70 × 0.53). Musée National d'Art Moderne. Paris. Ph. Réunion des Musées Nat. © Spadem 1983.
170 1. Honoré Daumier: *The Laundress.* Oil on wood (0.490 × 0.325). Initials b.r. Louvre. Paris. Ph. Giraudon.
2. Ph. Roger-Viollet.
3. André Gill: *Gervaise Counting the Linen.* Illustration for Zola's *The Dram-Shop.* 1878. Édition. Bibl. Nat. Paris. Arch. E.R.L.
4. Henri de Toulouse-Lautrec: *The Laundress,* 1889 (0.93 × 0.75). Coll. priv. Arch. E.R.L.
171 1. Pablo Picasso: *Woman Ironing,* 1904 (1.160 × 0.725). S.b.r. Solomon Guggenheim Museum, New York. Justin K. Tannhauser Coll. Ph. C. Guadagno and D. Heald. © Spadem 1983.
2. Edgar Degas: *Laundresses* c. 1884 (0.760 × 0.815). S.f.r. Musée du Jeu de Paume, Paris. Ph. Giraudon. © Spadem 1983.
3. Théophile Steinlen: *Laundresses.* S.b.r. Illustration for *Le Rire* Arch. E.R.L. © Spadem 1983.
4. Musée Montmartre. Ph. E.R.L.
5. Edgar Degas: *Laundresses Carrying Linen,* 1876-78 (0.46 × 0.61). S.b.r. Sachs Coll. New York. Ph. Giraudon. © Spadem 1983.
172 1. Henri Gervex: *Rolla,* 1878 (1.75 × 2.20). S.D.b.l. Musée des Beaux-Arts, Bordeaux. Ph. Bulloz.
2. Ph. Braquehars, 1854. Bibl. Nat. Paris. Arch. E.R.L.
3. Edgar Degas: *Semi-Nude Woman Lying On her Back,* Black pencil shaded off (0.228 × 0.355). S.b.r. Louvre, Paris. Ph. Réunion des Musées Nat. © Spadem 1983.
173 1. Pierre Bonnard: *The Lovers* (0.195 × 0.270). S.b.l. Kunstmuseum Winterthur. © Spadem 1983.
2. Pierre Bonnard: *Indolent,* c. 1899 (0.92 × 1.08). Stamp b.l. Bowers Coll. Paris. © Spadem 1983.
3. Pablo Picasso: *The Embrace,* 1905. S.D. Dedicated: "To my dear friend, Guillaume Apollinaire." Private Coll. Paris. Arch. E.R.L. © Spadem 1983.
174 1. Henri de Toulouse-Lautrec: *The Dram-Shop,* 1900, Panel (0.55 × 0.43). Monogram b.r. Coll. Mrs. Florence Gould. Arch. E.R.L.
2. Théophile Steinlen: *Rue Caulaincourt.* S.b.r. Bibl. Nat. Paris. Arch. E.R.L. © Spadem 1983.
3. Jean-Louis Forain: *English Café.* Illustration for *Le Rire.* S.b.r. © Spadem 1983.
4. Ph. Seeberger.
175 1. Georges Rouält: *The Couple,* 1905. Watercolor (0.70 × 0.50). Private coll. Ph. Giraudon. © Spadem 1983.
2. Henri de Toulouse-Lautrec: *Laundress.* For the Courier Français. June 2, 1889 (0.34 × 0.23). Musée Henri de Toulouse-Lautrec, Albi. Ph. Giraudon.
3. Pablo Picasso: *Mother and Child in a Shawl,* 1903 (0.475 × 0.410). S.t.r. Picasso Museum, Barcelona. Ph. M.A.S. Barcelona. © Spadem 1983.
4. Ph. Seeberger.
5. Ph. Seeberger.
176 1. Théophile Steinlen: Poster for the *Reopening of the Chat Noir* cabaret, 1896. S.b.l. Coll. Romi. © Spadem 1983.
2. Auguste Géradin: *The Chat Noir Cabaret,* 1900. Coll. R. Dazy.
3. Ph. J. Warnod Collection.
4. Adolphe Willette: *Parce Domine!,* 1884 (4 × 2). S.b.r. Work executed in honor of the moving of the Chat Noir cabaret. Depot of the City of Paris. Ph. Musée Montmartre, Paris. © Spadem 1983.
177 1. Ph. Coll. Sirot-Angel.
2. Ph. Coll. Romi.
3. Henri de Toulouse-Lautrec: *Aristide Bruant.* Poster. S.b.l. Ph. H. Josse.
4. Théophile Steinlen: *Interior of Mirliton Cabaret.* Extract from *La Plume,* 1891. Coll. Romi. © Spadem 1983.
178 1. Edgar Degas: *Miss Lala at the Fernando Circus,* 1879 (1.170 × 0.775). S.b.l. National Gallery, London. Ph. Edimedia. © Spadem 1983.
2. Honoré Daumier: *Wrestlers,* 1852 (0.420 × 0.275). S.b.l. Ordrupgaardsamlingen, Copenhagen.
3. Henri de Toulouse-Lautrec: *The Flying Trapeze;* Circus drawing (0.500 × 0.325). Fogg Art Museum, Cambridge, Ma.
4. Musée Montmartre, Paris. Ph. E.R.L.
5. Ph. Coll. Sirot-Angel.
179 1. Pierre Bonnard: *Clown.* Pen and ink drawing. Monogram b.l. © Adagp 1983.
2. Ph. Coll. Villoteau.
3. Pablo Picasso: *Galloping Horse,* 1905. Pen and ink drawing. S.b.l. Baltimore Museum of Art. Cone Coll. © Spadem 1983.
4. Georges Seurat: *The Circus,* 1890-91 (1.855 × 1.525). Musée du Jeu de Paume, Paris Ph. Réunion des Musée Nat.
5. Henri de Toulouse-Lautrec: *At the Fernando Circus,* 1888 (50.98 × 1.61). Art Institute of Chicago. Joseph Winterbotham Coll.
180 1. Photo. Coll. Romi.
2. Max Jacob: *At the Circus,* 1912 (0.73 × 0.92). Musée du Petit Palais, Geneva.
3. Kees Van Dongen: *The Clown,* 1905-06. Oil on panel (0.74 × 0.60). S.b.r. Priv. Coll. © Spadem 1983.
4. Ph. Roger-Viollet.
5. Pierre-Auguste Renoir: *Clown,* 1868 (1.935 × 1.300). S.D.b.r. Rijkmuseum Kröller-Müller, Otterlo. © Spadem 1983.
181 1. Pablo Picasso: *Family of Acrobats with Monkey.* 1905 (1.05 × 0.75). S.t.r. Kunstmuseum, Göteborg. © Spadem 1983.
182 1. Vincent Van Gogh: *Woman with Tamborines,* 1887 (0.555 × 0.465). Vincent Van Gogh Museum, Amsterdam.
2. Henri de Toulouse-Lautrec: *A la Mie,* 1891. Watercolor and gouache on cardboard (0.53 × 0.68). S.t.r. Museum of Fine Arts, Boston.
3. Ph. Paul Sescau: Maurice Guilbert posing for *A la Mie.*
4. Henri de Toulouse-Lautrec: *Rice Powder,* 1889 (0.56 × 0.46). Vincent Van Gogh Museum, Amsterdam.
183 1. Vincent Van Gogh: *Open Air Café, Montmartre,* October 1886 (0.49 × 0.64). S.b.l. Musée du Jeu de Paume, Paris. Ph. Bulloz.
2. Pablo Picasso: *Woman Drinking Absinthe,* 1901. Hermitage Museum, Leningrad.
3. Paul Cézanne: *Card Players,* 1892-96 (0.470 × 0.565). Musée du Jeu de Paume, Paris. Arch. E.R.L.
184 1. Paul Gauguin: *Vision After the Sermon,* 1888. Detail. National Gallery of Scotland, Edinburgh.
185 1. Paul Gauguin: *Self Portrait with Yellow Christ,* c. 1889 (0.38 × 0.46). Coll. M. Denis Family, St-Germain-en-Laye. Ph. Giraudon.
190 1. Paul Gauguin: *Bonjour, M. Gauguin,* 1889 (0.740 × 0.546). Armand Hammer Foundation, Los Angeles.
191 1. Camille Pissarro: *Portrait of Gauguin,* Pastel and pencil. Musée du Jeu de Paume, Paris. Ph. Réunion des Musées Nat.
2. Ph. Arch. E.R.L.
3. Ph. Arch. E.R.L.
4. Paul Gauguin: *Breton Landscape with David Mill* (0.73 × 0.92). S.b.r. Musée du Jeu de Paume, Paris. Réunion des Musées Nat.
5. Ph. Coll. Luc Robin. Atelier de l'Aven.
192 1. Ph. Coll. Luc Robin. Atelier de l'Aven.
2. Ph. Coll. Luc Robin. Atelier de l'Aven.
3. Émile Jourdan: *Rue de Concarneau at Pont-Aven.* S.b.r. Coll. priv. Ph. G. Perron. E.R.L.
4. Ph. Coll. Luc Robin. Atelier de l'Aven.
5. Paul Gauguin: *Still Life with Ham,* 1889 (0.50 × 0.58). Initials c.r. Phillips Coll. Washington D.C.
193 1. Paul Gauguin and Émile Bernard: *Sculpted Cupboard.* Polychrome. Private Coll. Arch. E.R.L.
2. Ph. Roger-Viollet.
3. Paul Gauguin: *The White Table Cloth. Pension Gloanec,* 1886 (0.55 × 0.58). S.D.b.r. Ph. Christie's London.
194 1. Émile Bernard: *Yellow Tree,* c. 1888 (0.660 × 0.365). Musée des Beaux-Arts, Rennes. © Spadem 1983.
2. Ph. Arch. E.R.L.
3. Maurice Denis: *Sunlight on the Terrace,* 1890. Oil on cardboard (0.200 × 0.200). D.b.r. D. Denis Coll. St-Germain-en-Laye. Ph. Giraudon. © Spadem 1983.
195 1. Paul Sérusier: *The Talisman,* October 1888. Oil on wood (0.270 × 0.220). Coll. M. Denis Family, Alençon. Ph. Giraudon. © Spadem 1983.
196 1. Émile Bernard: *Bretons in a Green Meadow,* 1888 (0.74 × 0.92). S.D.b.l. Coll. M. Denis Family, St-Germain-en-Laye.
2. Ph. Coll. Sirot-Angel.
3. Ph. Coll. Satre Family.
4. Paul Gauguin: *The Belle Angèle,* 1889 (0.92 × 0.72). S.D.b.l. Musée du Jeu de paume, Paris. Ph. Réunion des Musées Nat.
197 1. Vincent Van Gogh: *Dance Hall at the Folies Arlésiennes,* 1888 (0.64 × 0.80). Musée du Jeu de Paume, Paris. Ph. Réunion des Musées Nat.
2. Ph. Coll. Pierre Richard.
3. Vincent Van Gogh: *Old Woman of Arles* (0.55 × 0.43). Vincent Van Gogh Museum, Amsterdam.
198 1. Paul Sérusier: *Solitude,* 1890-92 (0.75 × 0.50). Musée des Beaux-Arts, Rennes. © Spadem 1983.
2. Ph. Bibl. Nat. Paris.
3. Jan Verkade: *Breton Woman,* 1892. Drawing (0.28 × 0.20). Jan Bredholt Coll. Klampenborg.
4. Ph. Arch. E.R.L.
5. Pierre Puvis de Chavannes: *Young Girls at the Sea Shore,* 1879 (2.05 × 1.54). S.D.b.l. Louvre, Paris. Ph. Réunion des Musées Nat.
199 1. Émile Bernard: *Madeline in the Bois d'Amour,* 1888 (1.37 × 1.64). S.D.b.l. Pont-Aven. Musée d'Art Moderne, Paris. Ph. Réunion des Musées Nat.
2. Paul Gauguin: *Loss of Virginity or The Awakening of Spring,* 1891 (0.90 × 1.30). Chrysler Art Museum, Norfolk. Ph. Bulloz.
200 1. Paul Gauguin: *Breton Calvary,* 1889 (0.92 × 0.73). S.b.l. Musées Royaux des Beaux-Arts, Brussels.
2. Ph. G. Perron. E.R.L.
3. PMh. G. Perron. E.R.L.
4. Ph. G. Perron. E.R.L.
5. Charles Filiger: *Christ at Landes.* Gouache (0.300 × 0.210). S.b.r. Private Coll. Ph. G. Perron. E.R.L.
201 1. Paul Gauguin: *Yellow Crucifix,* 1889 (0.92 × 0.73). S.D.b.r. Albright-Knox Art Gallery, Buffalo. New York.
202 1. Albert Charpentié: *World's Fair, 1889.* General view of the Champs de Mars from one of the towers at Trocadero. Engraving. Ph. Bibl. Nat. Paris.
2-3. Catalogue of the Exhibition at Café Volponi, 1889. Title page. Illustration by paul Gauguin: *The Black Rocks.* Archives Ides et Calendes.
4. Catalogue of Exhibition at Café Volponi, 1889. Illustration by Émile Bernard: *Synthesism.* Left to right: Schuffenecker, E. Bernard, Gauguin. Louvre, Paris. Cbt. des Dessins. Ph. Réunion des Musées Nat. © Spadem 1983.
5. Catalogue of Exhibition at Café Volponi, 1889. Illustration by Émile Bernard: *Dreaming.* Archives Ides et Calendes. © Spadem 1983.
203 1. Paul Gauguin: *The Schuffenecker Family,* 1889 (0.73 × 0.92). Dedication b.r. "In memory of the good Schuffenecker". Musée du Jeu de Paume, Paris. Ph. Réunion des Musées Nat.
2. Catalogue of Exhibition at Café Volponi, 1889. Illustration by Émile Schuffenecker: *Women Gathering Seaweed.* Archives Ides et Calendes.

3. Catalogue of the Exhibition at the Café Volponi, 1889. Illustration by paul Gauguin: *Haymakers.* Archives Ides et Calendes.

204 1. Ph. Coll. Gourrier.
2. Ph. Coll. Le Thoer.
3. Charles Filger: *Breton Landscape. Pouldu*, c. 1897. Gouache (0.260 × 0.385). Ph. Galerie Daniel Malingue, Paris.
4. Ph. Arch. E.R.L.
5. Meyer de Haan: *Women Grinding Hemp*, 1889. Fresco mounted on canvas (1.33 × 2.01). Ph. Sotheby's, London.

205 1. Paul Gauguin: *Head of Meyer de Haan*, 1889. Sculpted oak (0.695 × 0.298). Private Coll. Archives Ides et Calendes.
2. Jacob Meyer de Haan: *Motherhood: Marie Henry Feeding her Child* (Marie Poupée and her baby), 1891 (0.73 × 0.60). Josefowitz Coll. Switzerland.
3. Maurice Denis: *Mother and Child*, 1895 (0.428 × 0.344). S.D.t.l. Oil on cardboard remounted on wood. Musée des Beaux-Arts, Rennes.

206 1. Paul Sérusier: *Pont-Aven Triptych*, c. 1892-93 (0.730 × 1.330). Galerie Jean-Claude Bellier, Paris. Ph. J. Warnod Coll. © Spadem 1983.

208 1. Paul Gauguin: *Breton Landscape with a Dog*, 1889 (0.925 × 0.735). S.D.b.r. R. Staechelin Coll. Basel. Ph. Hinz.
2. Charles Filiger: *Portrait of Young Breton Fisherman.* Gouache on cardboard (0.262 × 0.182). S.b.r. Private Coll. Ph. G. Demais. E.R.L.
3. Ph. Coll. D. Andred.
4. Paul Gauguin: *Isolated House, Brittany*, 1889 (0.600 × 0.735). S.D.b.r. Private Coll. New York.

209 1. Charles Filiger: *House of the Hanged Man I* (On reverse n° 16; allegorical landscape). Gouache on cardboard (0.180 × 0.204). S.b.l. Ph. Studio Lourmel, Paris.
2. Ph. Gourrier Coll.

210 1. Ph. G. Perron. E.R.L.
2. Henry Moret: *Houat Island*, 1893 (0.65 × 0.54). S.D.b.l. Private Coll. Ph. G. Perron. E.R.L.
3. Jacob Meyer de Haan: *Farm with Wells, Pouldu*, 1889 (0.735 × 0.930). S.D.b.l. Rijksmuseum Kröller-Müller, Otterlo.
4. Ph. Private Coll. Arch. E.R.L.

211 1. Paul Gauguin: *The Gate*, 1889 (0.92 × 0.73). S.b.r. Private Coll. Zurich. Ph. Bulloz.
2. Ph. Marie-José Drogon Collection.
3. Cuno Amiet: *Violet Calf in a Field*, Tempera on canvas (0.685 × 1.230). Monogram D.B.r. Kunstmuseum Olten. Ph. Wolf. A.G.

212 1. Henry Moret: *Rolling at Pouldu*, 1894 (0.580 × 0.720). S.d.b.l. Private Coll. Ph. G. Perron. E.R.L.
2. Wladyslaw Slewinski: *Boy with Red Flower*, 1890 (0.34 × 0.20). S.b.r. Private Coll. Ph. G. Perron. E.R.L.
3. Ph. Marie-José Drogon Collection.

213 1. Paul Sérusier: *Washerwomen at Bellangenet*, 1892 (0.54 × 0.65). Private Coll. Ph. G. Perron. © Spadem 1983.
2. Ph. G. Perron. E.R.L.
3. Paul Sérusier: *Filiger's House at Lannmarch*, c. 1890 (0.380 × 0.574). Monogram b.r. Private Coll. Ph. G. Perron. E.R.L. © Spadem 1983.

214 1. Photo. Arch. E.R.L.
2. Charles Filger: *Breton Youths*, 1890. Gouache on cardboard (0.208 × 0.170). Private Coll. Archives *Le Bateau Lavoir*, Paris.
3. Ph. G. Perron. E.R.L.
4. Ph. G. Perron. E.R.L.
5. Charles Filger: *Christ with Angels*, 1892. Gouache heightend with gold on cardboard (0.269 × 0.249). S.D.t.r. Coll. Mr. & Mrs. Arthur G. Altschul, U.S.A. Musée du Prieuré, St-Germain-en-Laye. Ph. Ph. Routhier. Studio Lourmel.

215 1. Charles Filiger: *Breton Cow Herder*, Gouache (0.395 × 0.165). S.b.l. Josefowitz Collection. Switzerland.
2. Charles Filiger: *Fisherman's Family*, 1894. Gouache on cardboard. S.b.r. Private Coll. Ph. G. Perron. E.R.L.
3. Charles Filger: *The Wandering Jew.* Presumed self portrait. Priv. Coll. Ph. G. Demais. E.R.L.

216 1. Paul Sérusier: *Gauguin Playing the Accordian*, 1890. Pencil. Mlle Boutaric Coll. Ph. Marc Vaux. © Spadem 1983.
2. Ph. Le Thoer Coll.
3. Paul Gauguin: *Breton Girls* (0.720 × 0.910). S.D.b.l. Neue Pinakothek, Munich. Ph. Bavaria Verlag.
4. Ph. Marie-José Drogon Coll.

217 1. Maurice Denis: *The Guidel Pardon* (0.72 × 0.91). Painting offered to Mme Sérusier as wedding gift. Arch. Ides et Calendes. © Spadem 1983.
2. Ph. Le Thoer Coll.
3. Jens Ferdinand Willumsen: *Breton Women*, 1890 (1.00 × 1.00). S.D.b.r. J.F. Willumsen museum, Frederikssund.

218 1. Maxime-Louis-Maufra: *Pont-Aven Landscape* (1.50 × 3.00). S.b.r. Musée des Beaux-Arts, Quimper. Ph. M. Le Grand. © Adagp 1983.
2. Ph. Marie-José Drogon Coll.
3. Charles Filiger: *Young Breton Seated on the Beach.* Gouache on cardboard. Ph. Gallerie Daniel Malingue, Paris.
4. Paul Gauguin: *Aita Aramoe.* Pastel (0.30 × 0.42). Dedicated "To my friend Maufra, avant-guard artist." S.b.r. Arch. Ides et Calendes.
5. Jan Verkade: *Young Breton on the Beach*, c. 1892-94 (0.30 × 1.00). S.b.r. Esther Bredholt Coll., Klampenborg. © Spadem 1983.

219 1. Maurice Denis: *Breton Regatta*, 1892. Monogram b.r. D. Denis Coll. St-Germain-en-Laye. Ph. Giraudon. © Spadem 1983.

220 1. Pablo Picasso: *Sketch for Demoiselles d'Avignon*, 1907 (1.19 × 0.93).S.b.r. Ernest Beyeler Coll., Basel. Ph. Galerie Beyeler. © Spadem 1983.

221 1. Pablo Picasso: *Self Portrait*, 1906 (0.905 × 0.710). S.D.b.l. Philadelphia Museum of Art. Coll. A.E. Gallatia. Arch. E.R.L. © Spadem 1983.

226 1. Musée Montmartre, Paris. Ph. E.R.L.
2. Musée Montmartre, Paris. Ph. E.R.L.
3. Ph. J. Warnod Coll.
4. Ph. Roger-Viollet.
5. Maurice Utrillo: *The Lapin Agile, Montmartre*, 1913 (0.57 × 0.76). S.D.b.r. Ph. Galerie Daniel Malingue, Paris. © Spadem 1983.
6. Pablo Picasso: *Père Frédé.* Study for the *Harlequin*. Ph. J. Warnod Coll. © Spadem 1983.

227 1. Pablo Picasso: *At the Lapin Agile (Harlequin with a Glass)*, 1905 (O.99 × 1.00). Payson Coll. New York. Ph. A. Held-Ziolo. © Spadem 1983.

228 1. Photo 1906. Archives of the Baltimore Museum of Art.
2. Ph. Roger-Viollet.
3. Pablo Picasso: *Gertrude Stein*, 1906 (1.00 × 0.81). Metropolitan Museum of Art, New York. G. Stein Bequest 1946. © Spadem 1983.

229 1. Ph. J. Warnod Coll.
2. Kees Van Dongen: *The Belle Fernande*, 1906 (1.00 × 0.81). S.b.l. Private Coll. Paris. Ph. Ides et Calendes. © Spadem 1983.
3. Photo 1906. J. Warnod Coll.
4. Photo. Dolly Van Dongen Coll.

230 1. André Warnod: *The Bateau-Lavoir.* Drawing. J. Warnod Coll. © Spadem 1983.
2. Ph. Bibl. Nat. Paris.
3. Ph. Izis, Paris-Match.
4. Ph. Bibl. Nat. Paris.

231 1. Juan Gris: *Place Ravignan.* Drawing. Musée Jacquemart-André, Paris. Ph. Coll. J. Warnod. © Spadem 1983.
2. Photo circa 1913, J. Warnod.
3. Juan Gris: *Woman* (Portrait of his wife Josette), 1917 (1.16 × 0.73). Private coll. Basel. Ph. A. Held-Ziolo. © Spadem 1983.

232 1. Ph. Gelett Burgess, New York, 1908.
2. Photo 1910. J. Warnod Collection.
3. Pablo Picasso: *Nude Against Red Background*, 1906 (0.81 × 0.54). S.t.r. Musée Orangerie, Paris. Walter Guillaume Coll. Ph. Réunion des Musées Nat. © Spadem 1983.
4. Juan Gris: *Portrait of Picasso*, 1912. Signed and dedicated "Homage to Pablo Picasso" (0.74 × 0.93). Art Institute of Chicago. Ph. Giraudon. © Spadem 1983.

233 1. Paul Cézanne: *Three Bathers*, 1879-82 (0.58 × 0.54). Petit-Palais, Paris. Ph. Bulloz.
2. Maurice de Vlaminck: *Bathers*, c. 1906-07 (0.89 × 1.16). S.b.l. Private coll. Ph. Ides and Calendes. © Spadem 1983.
3. Ph. Hassia.
4. Photo J. Warnod Coll.
5. Pablo Picasso: *Demoiselles d'Avignon*, 1907 (2.45 × 2.35). Museum of Modern Art, New York. Gift of Lillie P. Bliss. Ph. Giraudon. © Spadem 1983.
6. Museum of Art Catalonia. Ph. Arch. E.R.L.

234 1. Pablo Picasso: *Study or Demoiselles d'Avignon*, 1907 (0.22 × 0.17). Private Coll. Ph. Giraudon. © Spadem 1983.
2. Pablo Picasso: *Sketch for Demoiselles d'Avignon*, 1907. Watercolor (0.17 × 0.33). S.D.b.r. Philadelphia Museum of Art. A.E. Gallatin Coll. Ph. Alfred J. Wyatt. © Spadem 1983.
3. Photo 1907. Dolly Van Dongen Coll.
4. Ph. A. Held-Ziolo.

235 1. Pablo Picasso: *Demoiselles d'Avignon*, 1907 (2.45 × 2.35). Museum of Modern Art, New York. Gift of Lillie P. Bliss. Ph. Giraudon. © Spadem 1983.

236 1. Photo Archives Seghers.
2. Marie Laurencin: *Group of Artists*, 1908. Left to right: Picasso, Marie Laurencin, G. Apollinaire & Fernande Olivier (0.63 × 0.79). S.D.b.l. Baltimore Museum of Art. Carré Coll. © Adagp 1983.
3. Ph. Marouteau. Arch. Seghers.
4. Photo 1916. J. Warnod Coll.

237 1. Henri Rousseau: *The Muse Inspiring the Poet* (Portrait of G. Apollinaire & M. Laurencin), 1909 (1.46 × 0.97). S.b.r. Basel Museum. Ph. Giraudon.
2. Henri Rousseau: *Portrait of a Woman* (1.60 × 1.05). Louvre, Paris. Picasso Donation. Ph. Réunion des Musées Nat.
3. Pablo Picasso: *Portrait of Max Jacob*, Drawing on a Café-Brasserie Faurena stationary. 1904. Marcel Lecomte Coll. Paris. © Spadem 1983.
4. Photo, 1908. Hachette Photo-Library.

238 1. Photo, 1904. Coll. Sirot-Angel.
2. Ph. Studio Chevojon. © Spadem 1983.
3. Pablo Picasso: *Le Sacré Cœur*, 1909 (0.90 × 0.63). Private Coll. Ph. Giraudon. © Spadem 1983.
4. Georges Braque: *Le Sacré Cœur*, 1910 (0.555 × 0.410). S.D. on the back. Masurel Don. Musée d'Art Moderne du Nord, Villeneuve-d'Ascq. © Adagp 1983.

239 1. Maurice Utrillo: *Rue Chappe*, c. 1912. Diana Esmond Coll. New York. Arch. E.R.L. © Spadem 1983.
2. Photo Seeberger.
3. Suzanne Valadon: *The Sacred Heart Seen From the Garden at rue Cortot*, 1916 (0.63 × 0.53). Musée d'Art Moderne, C.N.A.C., Paris. Ph. Réunion des Musées Nat. © Adagp 1983.

240 1. Amedeo Modigliani: *Portrait of Paul Guillaume.* S. dedicated. D.b.l. © Adagp 1983.
2. Photo. 1912. Coll. L'Œil.
3. Photo, 1906. Coll. Sonia Delaunay.
4. Kees Van Dongen: *Portrait of Kahnweiler*, 1907 (0.65 × 0.54). S.t.r. Musée du Petit-Palais, Geneva. © Spadem 1983.
5. Robert Delaunay: *Portrait of Wilhem Uhde*, 1907 (0.80 × 0.65). S.b.r. Priv. Coll. © Adagp 1983.
6. Pablo Picasso: *Portrait of Daniel-Henri Kahnweiler*, 1910 (1.00 × 0.73). Art Institute of Chicago. Gift of Gilbert W. Chapman. © Spadem 1983.
7. Pablo Picasso: *Portrait of Wilhelm Uhde*, 1910 (0.81 × 0.60). Penrose Coll. London. Arch. E.R.L. © Spadem 1983.

241 1. Ph. Arch. E.R.L.
2. Paul Cézanne: *Portrait of Ambroise Vollard*, 1899 (1.03 × 0.81). Musée Petit-Palais, Paris. Ph. Giraudon.
3. Pablo Picasso: *Portrait of Amboise Vollard*, 1909-10 (0.92 × 0.65). Pushkin Museum, Moscow. Ph. Giraudon. © Spadem 1983.
4. Photo 1916. Museum of Modern Art, New York.

242 1. Ph. Coll. Sirot-Angel.
2. Georges Braque: *Side Table*, 1911 (0.72 × 0.795). Folkwang Museum, Essen. Ph. Giraudon. © Adagp 1983.
3. Jean Cocteau: *The Rotunde in 1915.* J. Warnod Collection. © Spadem 1983.

243 1. Pablo Picasso: *Bottle of "Old Marc"*, 1913. Charcoal and pasted paper (0.63 × 0.49). Musée National d'Art Modern Paris. Ph. Giraudon. © Spadem 1983.
2. Jean Mestzinger: *Still Life With a Pip* 1913 (0.35 × 0.27). S.B.l. Ph. R. Asse Geneva. © Adagp 1983.
3. Juan Gris: *Still Life: Bottle and Knif* 1912 (0.545 × 0.460). S.b.l. Rijksmuseum Kröller-Müller, Otterlo. © Spadem 1983.
4. Photo, 1910. Coill. The Rotonde.

244 1. Musée Montmartre, Paris. Ph. E.R.
2. Photo, 1900. Coll. The Rotonde.
3. Giorgio de Chirico: *Montparnas Train Station (Melancholy of Departure* 1914 (1.40 × 1.84). S.D.b.l. Museum Modern Art, New York, James Thra Soby Donation. © Spadem 1983.
4. Anton Kaminsky: *Corner of Avenue Maine and Boulevard de Vaugirard in 191* S.D.b.r. Ph. Coll. The Rotonde.

245 1. André Rouveyre: *Paul Fort.* Drawing Arch. Seghers.
2. Ph. Arch. Seghers.
3. André Warnod: *Apollinaire and Ma Jacob*. J. Warnod Coll. © Spadem 1983.
4. Juan Gris: *Man at a Café*, 1912 (1.22 0.88). S.b.l. Philadelphia Museum Art. Louise and Walter Arensberg Col © Spadem 1983.

246 1. André Lhote: Poster *"Evening Party Montparnasse"*, 1922. CNAC, Paris. Ph G. Demais. E.R.L. © Adagp 1983.
2. Ph. Roger-Viollet.
3. Sonia Terk Delaunay: *The Ball Bullie* 1913. Oil on ticking (0.97 × 3.90 S.D.b.r. Musée National d'Art Modern Paris. Ph. Réunion des Musées Nat. © Adagp 1983.
4. Francis Picabia: *Dance of Spring*, 191 (1.20 × 1.20). S.D.b.r. Philadelphia Museum of Art. Coll. Louise and Walte Arensberg. © Spadem 1983.

247 1. Gino Severini: *Blue Dancer*, 191 Coll. Private, Milan.
2. Photo. Collection of Closerie de Lila

248 1. Ph. Studio Limot.
2. Photo, 1906. J. Warnod Coll.
3. Fernand Léger: *Woman Sewing*, 190 Private Coll. Ph. Bulloz. © Spadem 198
4. Photo J. Warnod Coll.
5. Photo 1910. J. Warnod Coll.

249 1. Fernand Léger: *Nude in a Fores* 1909-11 (1.20 × 1.70). S.b.l. Rijksmuseum Kröller-Müller, Otterlo. © Spadem 1983.
2. Ph. Studio Limot.
3. Fernand Léger: *Smoke on Rooftop* 1912 (0.60 × 0.96). S.b.r. Minneapol Institute of Art. Putnam D. Mc Milla Collection. © Spadem 1983.

250 Marc Chagall: *Self Portrait with Seve Fingers*, 1912-13. S.D.b.l. (1.26 × 1.07 Stedelijk Museum, Amsterdam. © Adagp 1983.

251 1. Ph. Coll. Guy Selz.
2. Photo 1915. J. Kisling Collection.
3. Marc Chagall: *My Fiancée in Blac Gloves*, 1909 (0.88 × 0.64). S.D.b. Kunstmuseum Basel. Ph. Hinz. © Adagp 1983.
4. Moise Kispling: *Self Portrait with h Wife and Dog*, 1917 (1.16 × 0.87). Co J. Kisling. Ph. G. Demais. E.R.L. © Adagp 1983.

252 1. Ph. Yankel Collection.
2. Paul Krémègne: *The Beehive. Madam Oustroun's House.* S.b.r. Yandel Coll. © Adagp 1983.
3. Paul Krémègne: *Self Portrait.* S.b. Yankel Coll. © Adagp 1983.
4. Ph. Yankel Collection.
5. Michel Kikoine: *The Beehive Covere in Snow*, 1913-14 (0.43 × 0.33). S.b. Musée du Petit-Palais, Geneva. © Adag 1983.

253 1. Photo, 1914. Yankel Collection.
2. Michel Kikoine: *Self Portrait* (1.00 0.65). S.b.r. Mr. Himan Brown Col New York. Ph. Coll. Yandel. © Adag 1983.
3. Chaim Soutine: *Turkey and Tomatoe* Series begun in 1925 (0.81 × 0.49). S.b. Louvre, Paris. Walter Guillaume Col Ph. Giraudon. © Spadem 1983.
4. Photo, 1912-20. J. Warnod Coll.
5. Michel Kikoine: *Portrait of Soutine* S.b.r. Yankel Coll. © Adagp 1983.

254 1. Photo, Arch. E.R.L.
2. Amedeo Modigliani: *Portrait of Blais Cendrars*, 1917 (0.61 × 0.50). Coll. Gual

no, Rome, Arch. E.R.L. © Adagp 1983.
3. Marc Chagall: *Homage to Apollinaire,* 1911-12 (1.09 × 1.98). S.t.c. Stedelijk Van Abbe Museum, Eindhoven. Ph. Hinz-Ziolo. © Adagp 1983.
4. Pablo Picaso: *Picasso-Apollinaire Toasting,* 1918. J. Warnod Coll. © Spadem 1983.

255 1. Robert Delaunay: *Portrait of Guillaume Apollinaire,* 1911-12 (1.00 × 0.75). Musée d'Art Moderne. CNAC, Paris. Delaunay Donation 1963. Ph. Réunion des Musées Nat. © Adagp 1983.
2. Ph. Roger-Viollet, 1914.
3. Louis Marcoussis: *Portrait of Guillaume Apollinaire,* 1912. Etching (0.49 × 0.27). Philadelphia Museum of Art. Louise and Walter Arensberg Coll. Arch. E.R.L. © Spadem 1983.
4. Giorgio de Chirico: *Portrait of Guillaume Apollinaire,* 1914. Oil and charcoal on canvas (0.815 × 0.650). S.d.b.r. Musée National d'Art Moderne. CNAC, Paris. Ph. Réunion des Musées Nat. © Spadem 1983.
5. Jean Metzinger: *Study for portrait of Apollinaire,* 1911 Drawing (0.12 × 0.10). Bibl. Nat. Paris. Ph. E.R.L. © Adagp 1983.
6. Amedeo Modigliani: *Portrait of Guillaume Apollinaire,* 1917. Graphite drawing. Arch. Seghers. © Adagp 1983.

256 1. Photo, Dolly Van Dongen Collection.
2. Kees Van Dongen: *The Red Dancer,* 1907 (0.99 × 0.80). S.b.l. Hermitage Museum, Leningrad. Ph. Giraudon. © Spadem 1983.
3. Ph. E. Deletang, 1913. J. Warnod Coll.

257 1. Photo, 1913. Arch. E.R.L.
2. Tsugouharu Foujita: *Nude Combing Her Hair,* Drawing (0.48 × 0.65). Musée de Petit Palais, Geneva. © Adagp 1983.
3. Photo. 1920-22. Guy Krogh Coll.
4. Jules Pascin: *Resting.* Coll. Sarah & Abel Rambert, Paris. Ph. G. Demais. E.R.L. © Spadem 1983.
5. Jules Pascin: *Young Girl in Pink,* 1912. Coll. Sarah & Abel Rambert, Paris. Ph. G. Demais. E.R.L. © Spadem 1983.

258-259 Amedeo Modigliani: *Sleeping Nude,* 1917 (0.60 × 0.92). S.t.r. Private Coll. Museum of Modern Art Milan. Ph. Rizzoli Editore. © Adagp 1983.

260 1. Ph. Arch. E.R.L.
2. Jeanne Hébuterne: *Self Portrait,* 1916. Oil on cardboard (0.50 × 0.35). S.t.l. Musée du Petit Palais, Geneva.
3. Amedeo Modigliani: *Portrait of Jeanne Hébuterne,* 1919 (0.92 × 0.54). S.t.r. Coll. private. Ph. Giraudon. © Adagp 1983.
4. Amedeo Modigliani: *Nude Sleeping on Left Side* (0.89 × 1.46). S.b.l. Private Coll. Arch. E.R.L. © Adagp 1983.

5. Henri Rousseau: *The Dream,* 1910 (2.04 × 2.98). S.D.b.r. Museum of Modern Art, New York. Nelson A. Rockerfeller Donation.
6. Kees Van Dongen: *Tranquility,* 1918 (1.46 × 1.14). S.c.r. Private Coll. © Spadem 1983.

261 1. Henri Matisse: *The Dance,* 1910 (2.60 × 3.91). Hermitage Museum, Leningrad. Former coll. S. Chtchoukine. ©Spadem 1983.
2. Moïse Kisling: *Nude on a Red Sofa,* 1918 (0.60 × 0.73). Musée du Petit Palais, Geneva. © Adagp 1983.

262 1. Moïse Kisling: *Jean Cocteau Seated in the Studio,* 1916 (0.73 × 0.60). S.D.b.l. Musée du Petit Palais, Geneva. © Adagp 1983.
2. Amedeo Modigliani: *Portrait of Artist by Himself,* 1919 (1.00 × 0.65). S.t.r. Jolanda Penteado Montarazzo. Coll. Saõ Paulo. Arch. E.R.L. © Adagp 1983.
3. Tullio Garbari: *Intellectuals at the Rotonde,* 1916. LEft: Marinetti, center: Apollinaire, behind standing: Bayer, seated at right. L. Blum; extreme left. A. Suarés (1.01 × 1.01). Musée du Petit Palais, Geneva.

263 1. Pablo Picasso: *Curtain for "Parade",* 1917 (10.60 × 17.25). Musée d'Art Moderne, Paris. Ph. Réunion des Musées Nat. © Spadem 1983.

2. Ph. J. Kisling Collection.
3. Photo, 1916. Archives Seghers.
4. Pablo Picasso: *Portrait of Erik Satie,* 1920. Graphite (0.62 × 0.48). D.b.r. Private Coll. Ph. Giraudon. © Spadem 1983.

264 1. Marcel Duchamp: *Nude Descending Staircase,* 1912 (1.47 × 0.88). T.b.r./ S.c.b. Philadelphia. Museum of Modern Art. Coll. Louise and Walter Arensberg. Arch. E.R.L. © Adagp 1983.
2. Robert Delaunay: *Windows Opening Simultaneously,* 1912 (0.46 × 0.37). D. dedicated b.r. Tate Gallery, London. Ph. John Webb. © Adagp 1983.
3. Fernand Léger: *The Card Game,* 1917 (1.29 × 1.93). S.D.b.r. Rijksmuseum Kröller-Müller, Otterlo Arch. E.R.L. © Adagp 1983.

265 1. Robert Delaunay: *Disc: First Nonobjective Painting,* 1912 (1.34 diameter). Coll. Mrs. Bruton Tremaine, Meriden, Conn. © Adagp 1983.
Tourist Guide
p. 267: see p. 42 (5). Photo D. Czap: p. 271 (3). Photos G. Demais-E.R.L.: p. 268, 269, 270, 273 (2-3), 276, 277, 278, 279 (1). Photo Giraudon: 279 (3). Photos G. Perron: p. 272 (1), 272 (3), 273 (1-4), 274, 275, 279 (2). P. Poullain-Normandie Photo Industrie: p. 270 (2), 271.

Acknowledgments

I would like to take this opportunity to thank all the people who were so eager to encourage, inform and assist me with this book. The number of those to whom I owe my gratitude is so great that I am obliged to simply list their names in alphabetical order. My special gratitude goes to Robert Laffont, François d'Esneval and the dynamic team at Editions Robert Laffont—these people believed in this book, produced it, promoted it and took charge of its distribution.

M. Ajame
Mme Angel-Sirot
M. & Mme Audren
Mme Bergeret
Mlle Bernard-Rousseau
M. & Mme Boelen
Mlle Bowers
Mlle Buquet
M. Cabanne
Mme Cazeau-Caille
Mme Cézanne
M. Charpentier
Mme Dedeban
Mme Fassano
M. Fohanno
M. & Mme Fontaine
Mme Frèrebeau

Mlle Gassies
Mme Gauthier
M. Goulvain
M. Guerlain
M. Guyot
M. Hogg
Mme Jacque
Mme Jacob
M. Jean
Mme Jégou
M. Kisling
M. Laclotte
M. L. Laffont
Mme Lalance
Mme Lampel
M. Le Tellier
M. Le Thoer

M. Liegibel
M. Malingue
Mme Manguin
M. Milan
M. Maufra
M. Oberthur
Mme Paillard
Mme Parère
M. Paressant
M. Pélissier
M. Perron
M. Peuchmaurd
M. Piguet
Mlle Pouzoullic
M. & Mme Rambert
M. Rheims
M. Richard

Mme Roger
Mme Rolland
M. Romi
M. Rosselet
M. Sagne
M. Tafanel
M. Terrasse
M. Toscas
M. Trohel
M. Trouplin
Mme Van Dongen
M. Van der Kemp
Mme Vernet
Mme Warnod
M. Wildenstein

I would also like to express my full gratitude to all the museum curators in France and abroad—and in particular to Madame Bergeret of the Musée Boudin in Honfleur—as well as the priests, mayors and municipal counselors, local cultural administrators for the towns and communities concerned. I also want to thank the directors of the art galleries and photographic archives whose help was generously given. I must also mention certain reference works which were indispensible in establishing a bibliography: the remarkable *Impressionism and Its Era* by Sophie Monneret (Denoël, 1978) and Le Robert *Universal Dictionary of Painting.* I must give my thanks also to Jeanine Warnod who provided me with important documentation which she had gathered on the *Bateau-Lavoir* and *The Ruche.*

Yann le Pichon

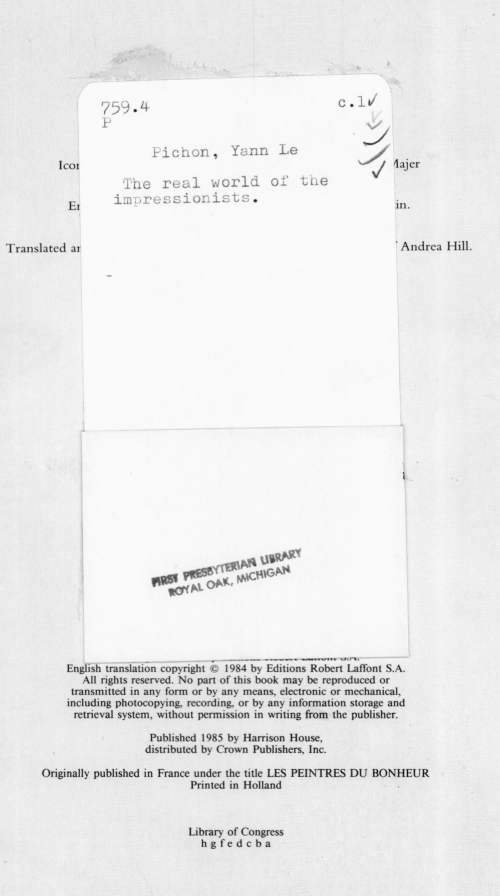

Icon ... Majer

En ... in.

Translated a ... Andrea Hill.

Published 1985 by Harrison House,
distributed by Crown Publishers, Inc.

Originally published in France under the title LES PEINTRES DU BONHEUR
Printed in Holland

Library of Congress
h g f e d c b a

ISBN 0-517-462672